Spring INTO GROWTH

A Social-Emotional Learning Workbook for Tweens

Ages 9 - 12

Fun Activities to Understand Your Feelings, Make Good Choices, and Grow This Spring!

RICHARD BASS

Note to Parents and Caregivers:

This workbook is designed for educational and personal development purposes for children ages 9-12. It is not intended as a substitute for professional mental health care, medical advice, diagnosis, or treatment. If your child is experiencing mental health concerns, trauma, or any condition that requires professional support, please consult with a qualified mental health professional, school counselor, or pediatrician.

The exercises and information in this workbook are based on evidence-informed practices in social-emotional learning and child development. Individual results may vary. The author and publisher are not responsible for any adverse effects or consequences resulting from the use of the suggestions or exercises in this book.

If your child is in crisis or you have concerns about their safety:
- **988 Suicide & Crisis Lifeline:** Call or text 988
- **Crisis Text Line:** Text HOME to 741741
- **Emergency Services:** Call 911

Note to Kids:

This workbook is YOUR space to learn about yourself, your feelings, and how to make good choices. There are no right or wrong answers—just YOUR answers. Have fun with it!

CONTENTS

Understanding Your Feelings and What Makes You Special

- *1.1 Spring Check-In: How Am I Feeling?*
- *1.2 My Feelings Thermometer*
- *1.3 What I Care About Most*
- *1.4 Things I'm Good At*
- *1.5 How My Body Talks to Me*
- *1.6 Draw Your Spring Self*
- *1.7 My Spring Promise to Myself*

Handling Big Feelings and Reaching Your Goals

- *2.1 What Stresses Me Out This Spring?*
- *2.2 Finishing the School Year Strong*
- *2.3 My Spring Goals*
- *2.4 Making Time for What Matters*
- *2.5 My Calm-Down Toolbox*
- *2.6 Sleep, Energy, and Feeling Good*
- *2.7 My Healthy Habits Tracker*

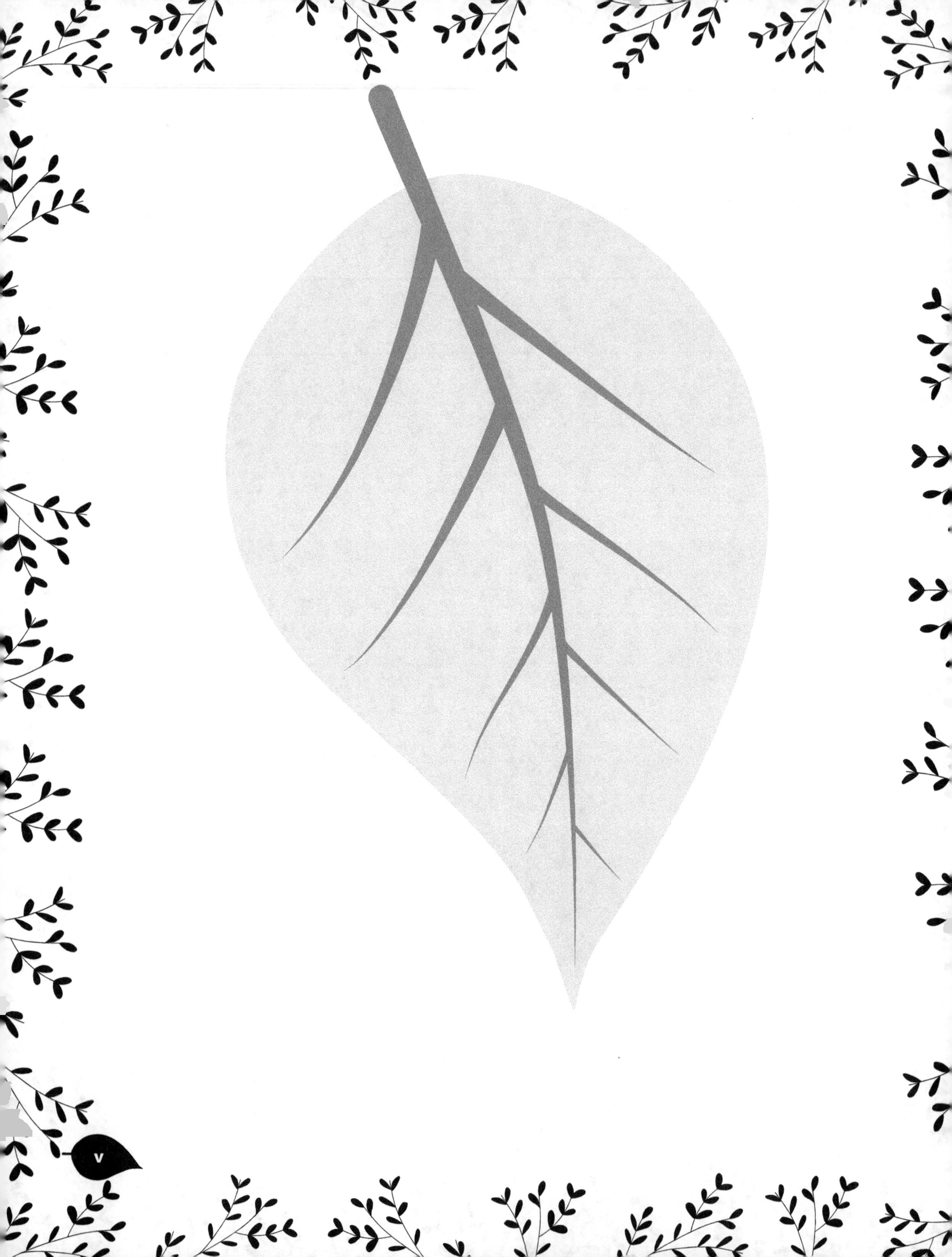

HOW TO USE THIS WORKBOOK

Hey there!

Welcome to your Spring workbook! This book is all about YOU—learning about your feelings, making good choices, getting along with others, and becoming the awesome person you already are!

What's Inside:

This workbook has **5 chapters** that teach you important skills:

1. **Self-Awareness** = Understanding yourself and your feelings

2. **Self-Management** = Being in charge of your emotions and reaching goals

3. **Social Awareness** = Understanding and caring about other people

4. **Relationship Skills** = Getting along with friends and family

5. **Responsible Decision-Making** = Making smart choices

How to Use It:

- **Option 1:** *Start at the Beginning*
    - Work through one activity at a time, from start to finish.

- **Option 2:** *Jump Around*
    - Pick whatever activity sounds fun or helpful right now!

- **Option 3:** *Do a Little Each Week*
    - Try to complete 2-3 activities per week throughout spring.

Important Stuff to Know:

✓ There are NO wrong answers—only YOUR answers
✓ You can use pencil and change your mind
✓ Skip activities that don't make sense for you
✓ You don't have to show anyone what you write unless you want to
✓ Some activities are quick (5 minutes), some take longer—go at your own pace
✓ You can draw, doodle, and make this book YOURS
✓ If something makes you feel upset or confused, talk to a grown-up you trust

What You Need:

Just you, something to write with, and an open mind! Some activities might need colored pencils or markers for the fun parts.

Let's Grow This Spring!

Spring is the perfect time to learn new things, try new activities, and grow (just like the flowers and trees outside). This workbook will help you grow on the INSIDE—becoming more confident, making better choices, and understanding yourself and others better.

Ready?
Let's go!

INTRODUCTION

YOUR SPRING ADVENTURE STARTS HERE!

Welcome to spring—one of the most exciting times of the year!

What's So Special About Spring?

Spring means:

- Flowers blooming and trees getting green again
- Warmer weather and more time outside
- Spring break and fun activities
- Getting close to the end of the school year
- New beginnings and fresh starts
- Spring sports, outdoor games, and adventures

But spring can also bring some tricky stuff:

- Stress about finishing the school year strong

- Wondering what you'll do over summer
- Friendship changes as the year ends
- Feeling pressure about grades or activities
- Dealing with big feelings about changes ahead

That's Where This Workbook Comes In!

This book teaches you five super-important skills that will help you handle all the good AND challenging parts of spring. These are called **Social-Emotional Learning (SEL)** skills, but don't let the big words scare you!

They're just skills that help you:

- Understand your feelings better
- Handle tough situations
- Get along with friends and family
- Make good choices
- Feel more confident and happy

The Five Skills You'll Learn:

1. Self-Awareness (Chapter 1)

This means knowing yourself—what you feel, what you're good at, what matters to you, and what makes you special.

2. Self-Management (Chapter 2)

This is about being in charge of your feelings and actions instead of letting them control you. You'll learn how to calm down when you're upset, reach your goals, and take care of yourself.

3. Social Awareness (Chapter 3)

This means understanding other people's feelings and caring about them, even when they're different from you.

4. Relationship Skills (Chapter 4)

These are the skills you need to make friends, keep friends, work with others, and solve problems when people don't get along.

5. Responsible Decision-Making (Chapter 5)

This is about making smart choices—thinking before you act, choosing what's right even when it's hard, and planning for the future.

Why These Skills Matter

Kids who learn these skills:

- Feel happier and more confident
- Do better in school
- Have better friendships
- Handle stress and tough times better
- Make choices they feel good about

And here's the really cool part: These aren't just *"school skills."* They help you your WHOLE LIFE— now, in middle school, in high school, and even when you're a grown-up!

How This Workbook Works

Each chapter has 7 activities that help you practice that skill. Some activities involve writing, some have you draw or create things, and some ask you to try new things in real life.

You can:

- Work through them in order
- Skip around to what sounds fun
- Take your time or zoom through
- Come back and do them again later

Your Spring Challenge

As you work through this book, challenge yourself to:

- Be honest (there are no wrong answers!)
- Try your best (even on hard activities)
- Have fun (this isn't homework—it's for YOU)
- Use what you learn in real life (that's where the magic happens!)

Let's make this a spring you'll remember—a spring where you learn about yourself, make good choices, and become even more amazing than you already are.

Turn the page and let's get started!

CHAPTER 1

SELF-AWARENESS

Knowing Yourself

> ❝ *"Knowing yourself is the beginning of all wisdom."* - **Aristotle**

What is Self-Awareness?

Self-awareness means understanding yourself—knowing how you feel, what you think, what you're good at, and what makes you special. It's like being a detective investigating the most interesting person in the world: YOU!

When you have good self-awareness, you can:

- Name your feelings instead of just feeling confused
- Know what you like and don't like
- Understand why you react the way you do
- Recognize what you're good at
- Know what's important to you

Why Does This Matter?

Imagine trying to ride a bike with your eyes closed. Pretty hard, right? That's kind of what life is like when you don't know yourself well. But when you DO know yourself, you can:

- Make better choices
- Feel more confident
- Explain your feelings to others
- Know what makes you happy
- Set goals that actually matter to you

What You'll Learn in This Chapter:

In this chapter, you'll explore who you are right now—this spring. You'll think about your feelings, what makes you special, what you care about, and what you want for yourself.

Remember:

There are no right or wrong answers. This is all about discovering the awesome person you are!

Let's go!

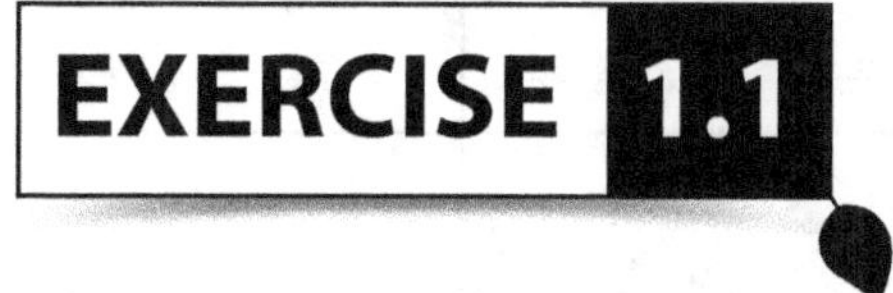

SPRING CHECK-IN - HOW AM I FEELING?

Spring is here! Let's check in on how you're feeling right now.

PART 1: QUICK FEELINGS CHECK

- *Circle or color in how you're feeling today:*

PART 2: SPRING FEELINGS

Question	Your Answer
One word to describe how I feel about spring:	
Something I'm excited about this spring:	
Something I'm worried about:	
The best thing happening right now:	

Something I wish was different:	
Who makes me feel happy:	

PART 3: IF I WAS...

Sometimes it's easier to describe feelings using comparisons. Fill in the blanks:

- *If my mood was weather, it would be:*

____

____

- *If my energy was an animal, it would be:*

____

____

- *If my feelings were a color, they'd be:*

____

____

PART 4: LOOKING AHEAD

- *By the end of spring, I want to feel:*

____

____

____

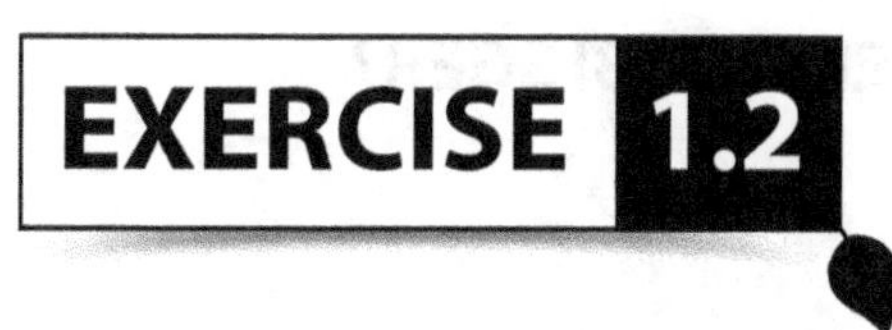

MY FEELINGS THERMOMETER

Just like a thermometer shows how hot or cold it is outside, a feelings thermometer shows how BIG or small your emotions are.

HOW IT WORKS:

Feelings aren't just *"on"* or *"off."* They come in different sizes! Understanding how big your feeling is can help you know what to do about it.

PRACTICE:

Where Are These Feelings Right Now?

Draw a line from each feeling to where it is on YOUR thermometer today:

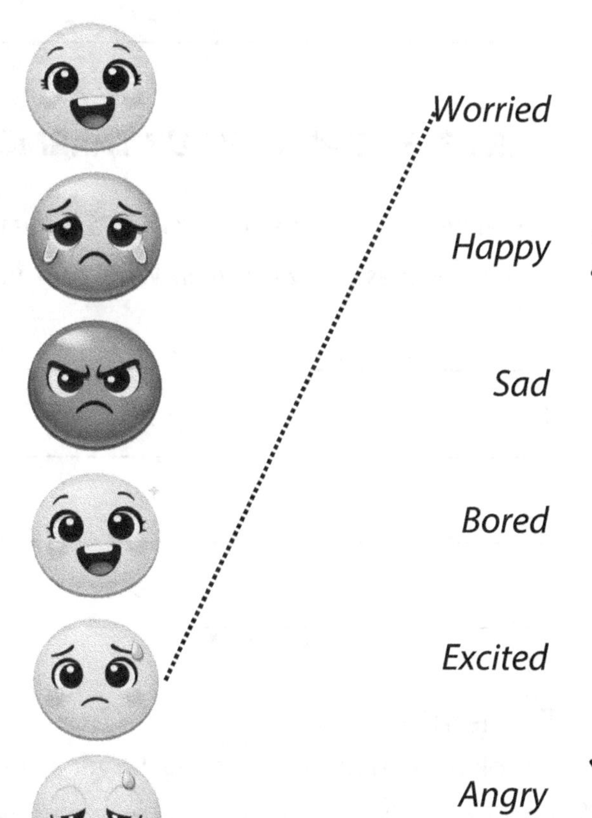

PART 2: WHAT MAKES FEELINGS BIGGER?

- *My worry gets bigger when:*

____

____

____

____

- *My anger gets bigger when:*

____

____

____

____

PART 3: KNOWING YOUR THERMOMETER

- *When my feelings hit Level 4 or 5, I can tell because:*
  (How does your body feel? What do you do?)

____

____

____

Remember:

It's okay to have BIG feelings! Everyone does. The important thing is knowing when they're getting too big and having ways to help yourself calm down (we'll work on that in Chapter 2!).

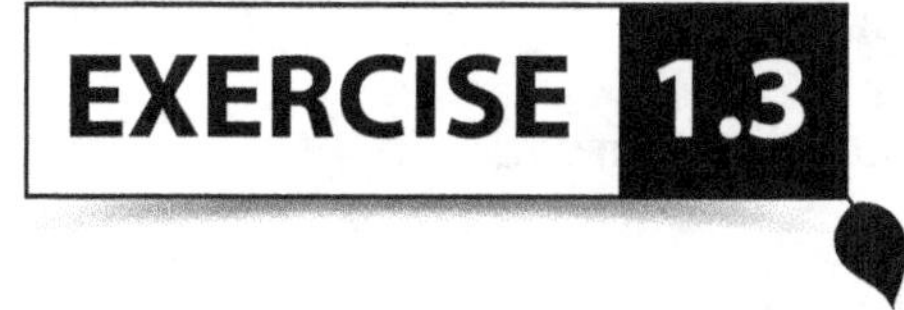

EXERCISE 1.3

WHAT I CARE ABOUT MOST

Values are the things that matter most to you—the stuff you think is really important. When you know your values, it's easier to make good choices!

PART 1: WHAT MATTERS TO ME?

Look at this list. Put a ⭐ next to the 5 things that matter MOST to you:

- Being kind to others
- Having fun
- Learning new things
- Being honest
- Having good friends
- Helping people
- Being creative
- Doing well in school
- Being fair
- Being brave

- Family time
- Being myself
- Staying healthy
- Trying my best
- Making people laugh
- Being a good friend
- Protecting nature
- Being respectful
- Having adventures
- Being organized

My Top 5 Values:

1. ____

2. ____

3. ____

4. ____

5. ____

PART 2: VALUES IN ACTION

Pick your #1 value from above. Let's explore it!

- *My #1 value is:*

____

____

____

- *I show this value when I:*

____

____

____

- *One way I can live this value MORE this spring:*

____

____

____

PART 3: WHEN VALUES ARE HARD

- *Sometimes it's hard to stick to my values when:*

____

____

Spring Challenge:

Pick one value and try to live it every day this week. Notice how it feels!

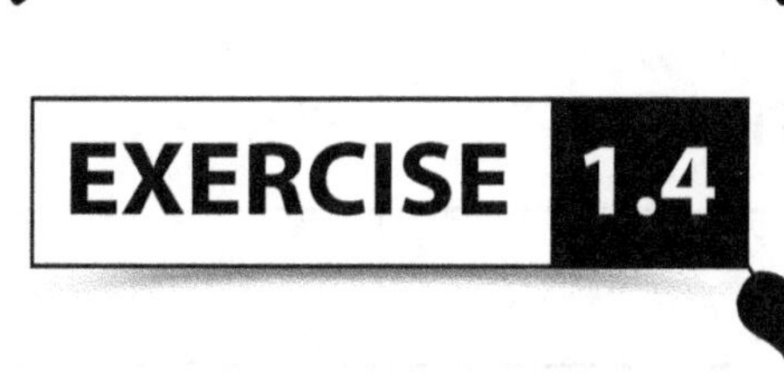

THINGS I'M GOOD AT

Everyone is good at something! Let's discover your strengths—the things you do well or that come naturally to you.

PART 1: STRENGTH HUNTER

Check off all the things you're good at (be honest—this isn't bragging, it's recognizing your awesomeness!):

SCHOOL STUFF:

☐ Math

☐ Reading

☐ Writing stories

☐ Science

☐ Art

☐ Music

☐ Following directions

☐ Asking good questions

☐ Memorizing things

☐ Solving problems

PEOPLE STUFF:

☐ Making friends

☐ Being a good listener

☐ Helping others

☐ Making people laugh

☐ Being kind

☐ Sharing

☐ Working in groups

☐ Standing up for others

☐ Cheering people up

PHYSICAL STUFF:

☐ Running fast

☐ Sports

☐ Dancing

☐ Building things

☐ Drawing/crafts

☐ Playing an instrument

☐ Coordination

☐ Being strong

PERSONAL STUFF:

☐ Being creative

☐ Staying calm

☐ Being organized

☐ Trying new things

☐ Not giving up

☐ Being honest

☐ Being brave

☐ Being responsible

☐ Being funny

☐ Being curious

PART 2: MY TOP STRENGTHS

My Strength	How I Use This
<u>Example:</u> I'm good at making people laugh	I tell jokes when my friends are sad

PART 3: STRENGTH STORY

- *Tell about a time when you used one of your strengths to do something good or solve a problem:*

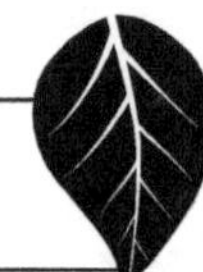

PART 4: GROWING A STRENGTH

- *Pick one strength you want to get even BETTER at this spring. How will you practice it?*

Remember:
Everyone has different strengths. That's what makes the world interesting! Your strengths are special and important.

EXERCISE 1.5

HOW MY BODY TALKS TO ME

Your body is really smart! It sends you signals about how you're feeling. Learning to listen to your body helps you understand yourself better.

PART 1: BODY FEELINGS MAP

On the body above, mark where you feel different emotions. Use different colors or symbols:

- 💜 *Happy/Excited (where do you feel this?)*
- 😟 *Worried/Nervous (where do you feel this?)*
- 😠 *Angry/Mad (where do you feel this?)*
- 😢 *Sad (where do you feel this?)*

Common body feelings:

- *Butterflies in stomach*
- *Tight chest*
- *Headache*
- *Tense shoulders*
- *Shaky hands*

- *Shaky hands*
- *Warm face*
- *Fast heartbeat*
- *Tired legs*

PART 2: WHEN I FEEL...

- *Looking at what bugs me, I notice that I get most upset when:*

Emotion	What My Body Does
Nervous	<u>Example:</u> My stomach feels funny and my hands get sweaty
Angry	
Happy	
Sad	
Excited	

PART 3: BODY SIGNALS

- *My body's way of telling me I'm stressed or upset is:*

____

____

____ 

____

- *When my body feels good and relaxed, I notice:*

____ 

____

PART 4: SPRING BODY CHECK

- *How does my body feel different in spring compared to winter?*
  (Think about: energy, sleep, allergies, how much you move)

Body Listening Tip:

Try checking in with your body once a day. Just notice: How do I feel? Where do I feel it? This helps you catch stress or upset feelings before they get too big!

DRAW YOUR SPRING SELF

Time to get creative! This is your chance to show who you are through art instead of just words.

INSTRUCTIONS:

In the space below, create a picture that shows YOU this spring. You can:

- Draw yourself doing something you love
- Use colors that represent your mood
- Include symbols of things that matter to you
- Add words or phrases that describe you
- Make patterns or designs that feel like *"you"*
- Draw your favorite spring things around you

There's no right or wrong way to do this! Just have fun!

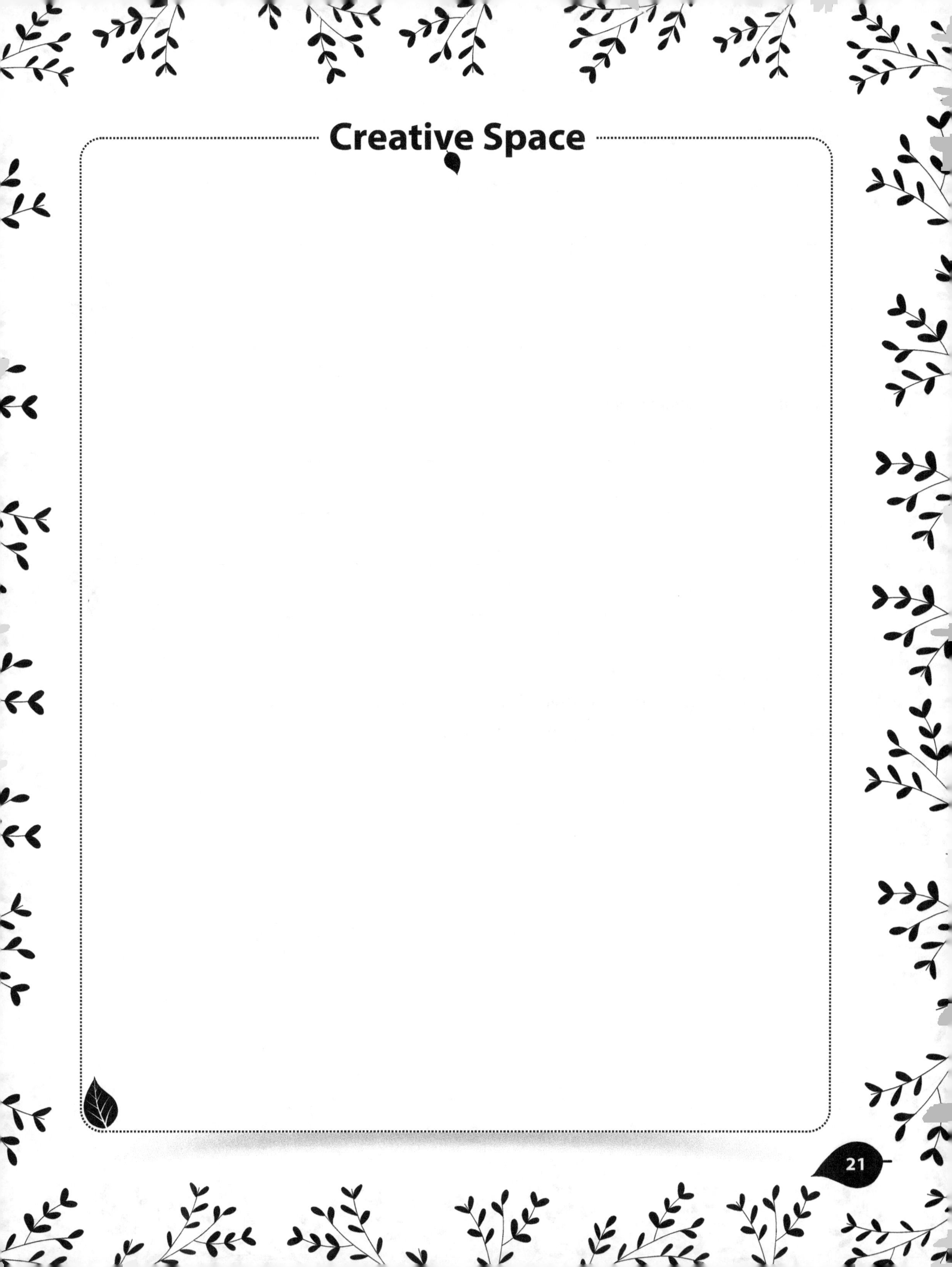

Creative Space

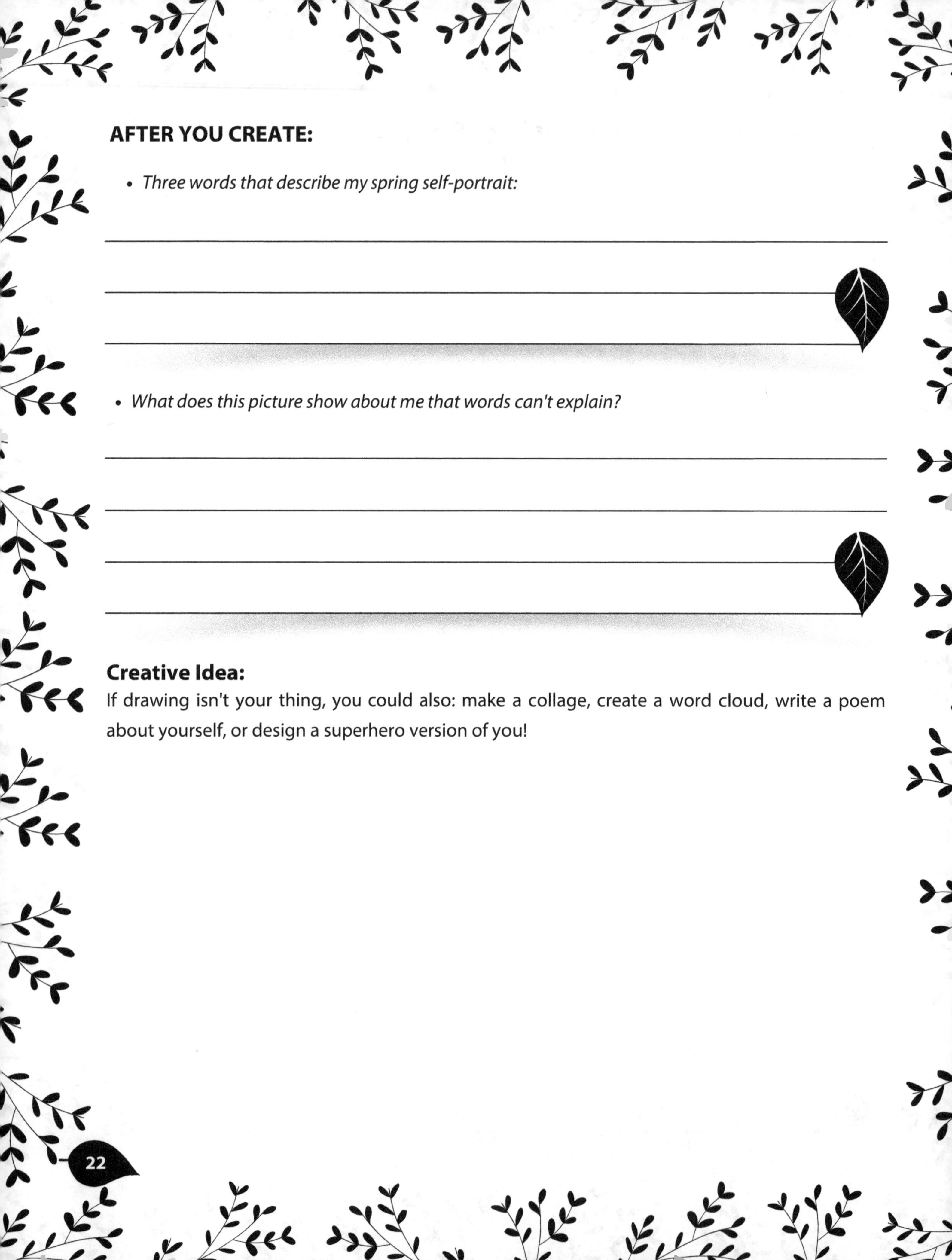

AFTER YOU CREATE:

- *Three words that describe my spring self-portrait:*

____

____

____

- *What does this picture show about me that words can't explain?*

____

____

____

Creative Idea:

If drawing isn't your thing, you could also: make a collage, create a word cloud, write a poem about yourself, or design a superhero version of you!

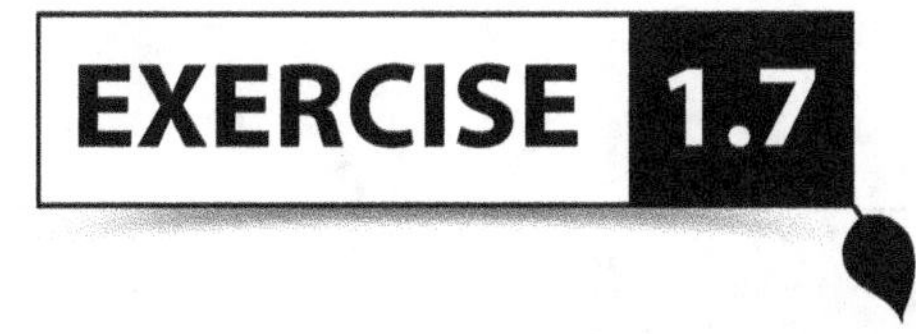

MY SPRING PROMISE TO MYSELF

A promise to yourself is a commitment about who you want to be and how you want to show up this spring.

PART 1: THIS SPRING, I WILL...

Fill in each promise:

- *This spring, I will be kind to myself by:*

____

____

- *This spring, I will try:*

____

____

- *This spring, I will NOT:*

____

____

- *This spring, I will spend more time:*

____

____

- *This spring, I will remember that:*

____

____

- *When things get hard this spring, I will:*

____

____

PART 2: MY SPRING PROMISE

Put it all together! Write your spring promise to yourself:

This spring, I promise to...

____

____

____

____

____

____

Signed:_____________________________

Date: _______________________________

MAKE IT SPECIAL:

Decorate this page! Use colors, stickers, drawings, make it something you'll want to look at all spring long.

Keep This Promise Visible:

Take a photo of this page or rewrite it on a poster to hang in your room!

END OF CHAPTER 1: SELF-AWARENESS

Great job! You just learned a LOT about yourself!

Before moving to Chapter 2, write down one cool thing you discovered about yourself:

____

____

____

____

➤ *Up Next: Chapter 2 - Self-Management*

Learn how to handle big feelings, reach your goals, and take care of yourself this spring!

CHAPTER 2

SELF-MANAGEMENT

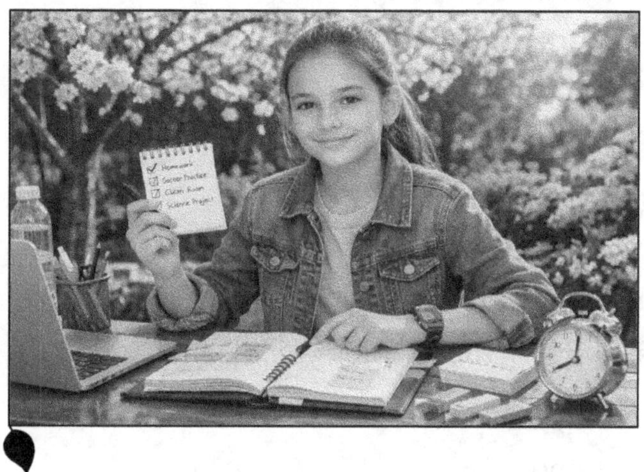

Being in Charge of You

What is Self-Management?

Self-management means being in charge of yourself—your feelings, your behavior, your time, and your choices. It's like being the boss of YOU!

When you're good at self-management, you can:

- Calm yourself down when you're upset
- Stick with something even when it's hard
- Set goals and actually reach them

- Make good choices about your time
- Take care of your body and mind

Why Does This Matter?

Imagine if every time you got mad, you just yelled and threw things. Or if every time something was hard, you just gave up. Life would be pretty rough, right?

Self-management helps you:

- Handle tough situations without melting down
- Reach goals that are important to you
- Feel more in control of your life
- Get along better with others
- Feel proud of yourself

What You'll Learn in This Chapter:

Spring can be busy and stressful! In this chapter, you'll learn how to:

- Figure out what's stressing you out
- Finish the school year strong
- Set and reach spring goals
- Manage your time better
- Build a toolbox of ways to calm down
- Create healthy habits

Remember:

Nobody's perfect at self-management. Even adults struggle sometimes! The goal is just to get a little better at it.

Let's get started!

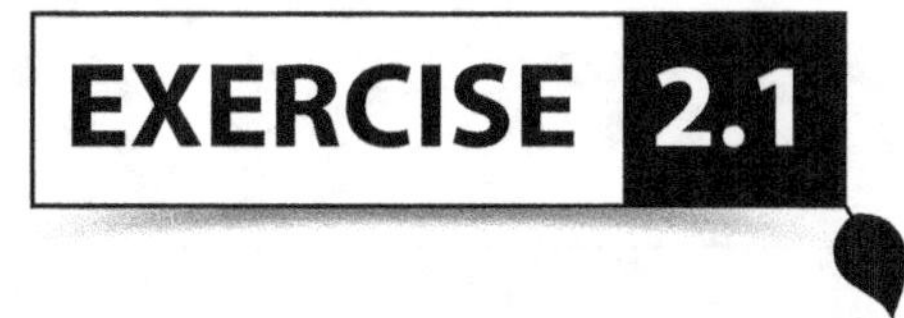

WHAT STRESSES ME OUT THIS SPRING?

Before you can manage stress, you need to know what's causing it!

PART 1: STRESS CHECK

- *How stressed do you feel right now? Circle one:*

Not stressed → **A little stressed** → **Medium stressed**→ **Pretty stressed**→ **VERY stressed**

PART 2: WHAT'S STRESSING ME OUT?

Put a check next to anything that's stressing you out this spring:

☐ Tests and schoolwork

☐ Grades

☐ Finishing projects

☐ Friend drama

☐ Not having enough friends

☐ Activities and sports

☐ Too much to do

☐ Not enough time

☐ Family stuff

☐ Worrying about summer

☐ Changes happening

☐ Not getting enough sleep

☐ Comparing myself to others

☐ Social media

☐ People being mean

☐ Trying to fit in

☐ Screen time arguments

☐ Chores and responsibilities

☐ Money worries

☐ Other: _______________________

My Top 3 Stresses:

1. ____

2. ____

3. ____

PART 3: HOW STRESS SHOWS UP

When I'm stressed...	This is what happens
My body feels:	<u>Example:</u> Tight stomach, headache, tired
I act:	
I think:	
Other people notice:	

PART 4: WHAT CAN I CONTROL?

Some stresses you CAN control. Some you CAN'T. Let's figure out which is which!

I CAN Control:
(Things I can change or do something about)

I CAN'T Control:
(Things I can't change)

_______________________   _______________________

_______________________   _______________________

<u>Example:</u> *How much I study*   <u>Example:</u> *What questions are on the test*

Smart Strategy:

Focus your energy on what you CAN control. For what you can't control, focus on how you REACT to it!

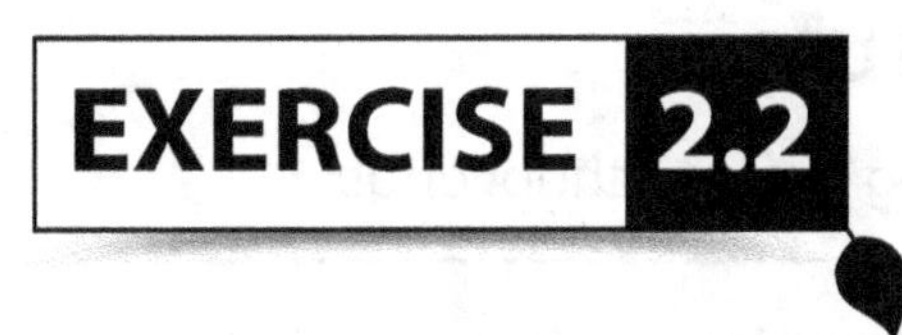

FINISHING THE SCHOOL YEAR STRONG

Spring means the school year is almost over! Let's make a plan to finish strong without getting too stressed.

PART 1: SCHOOL CHECK-IN

Subject	How I'm Doing (😊 Good / 😐 Okay / 😟 Struggling)	What I Need to Do

PART 2: WHAT'S COMING UP?

List important things happening before school ends:

What's Due/Happening	When
<u>Example:</u> Science project	May 15, 2026

PART 3: MY FINISH-STRONG PLAN

- *One thing I want to do better at before school ends:*

____

____

____

- *How I'll make this happen:*

____

____

____

PART 4: WHEN I NEED HELP

If I'm struggling with...	I can ask...
<u>Example:</u> Math homework	My teacher, parent, or friend who's good at math

PART 5: STAYING MOTIVATED

- *When school feels hard, I can remember:*

____

____

____

____

Pro Tip:

Break big tasks into small steps. Instead of *"finish science project,"* try *"work on project for 20 minutes."* Small steps are less scary!

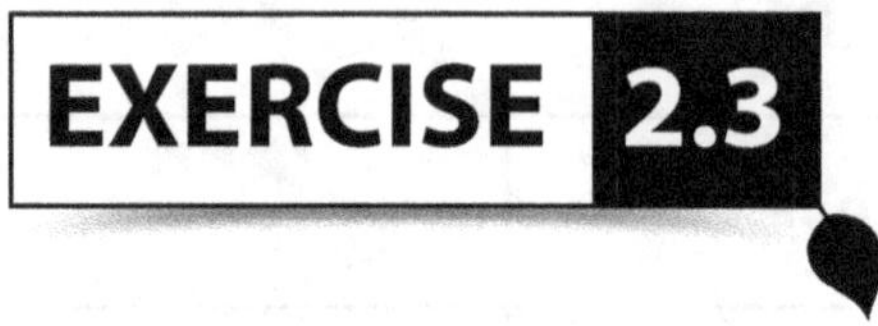

MY SPRING GOALS

Goals give you something to work toward! Let's set some spring goals that you can actually reach.

PART 1: WHAT DO I WANT?

- *Brainstorm! What would you like to do, learn, or accomplish this spring?*

____

____

____

____

PART 2: GOAL CATEGORIES

Pick 1-2 goals in different areas:

Category	My Goal
School	
Friends/Social	
Personal/Fun	
Health/Active	

PART 3: MAKE IT SMART

Pick your #1 goal and make it SMART:

- *Specific - Exactly what will you do?*
- *Measurable - How will you know you did it?*
- *Achievable - Is it realistic?*
- *Relevant - Does it matter to you?*
- *Time-bound - When will you do it by?*

My Goal:

____

____

- *Specific - What exactly will I do?*

____

____

- *Measurable - How will I know I reached it?*

____

____

- *Achievable - Can I really do this?*

____

____

- *Relevant - Why does this matter to me?*

____

____

- *Time-bound - When will I finish by?*

____

____

PART 4: ACTION STEPS

Break your goal into smaller steps:

Step	By When?
1	
2	
3	
4	

PART 5: WHAT MIGHT GET IN MY WAY?

- *Obstacles that might stop me:*

____

____

____

- *How I'll handle them:*

____

____

____

Goal Tip:

Tell someone about your goal! It helps you stay motivated when others know what you're working on.

MAKING TIME FOR WHAT MATTERS

There's so much to do in spring! Let's figure out how to make time for everything without feeling overwhelmed.

PART 1: WHERE DOES MY TIME GO?

On a normal day, about how much time do you spend on each thing?

Activity	Hours Per Day
Sleep	
School	
Homework	
Activities/Sports	
Screen time (TV, games, phone)	
Playing/Fun	
Family time	
Eating	
Getting ready (morning/night)	
Other: _________________	

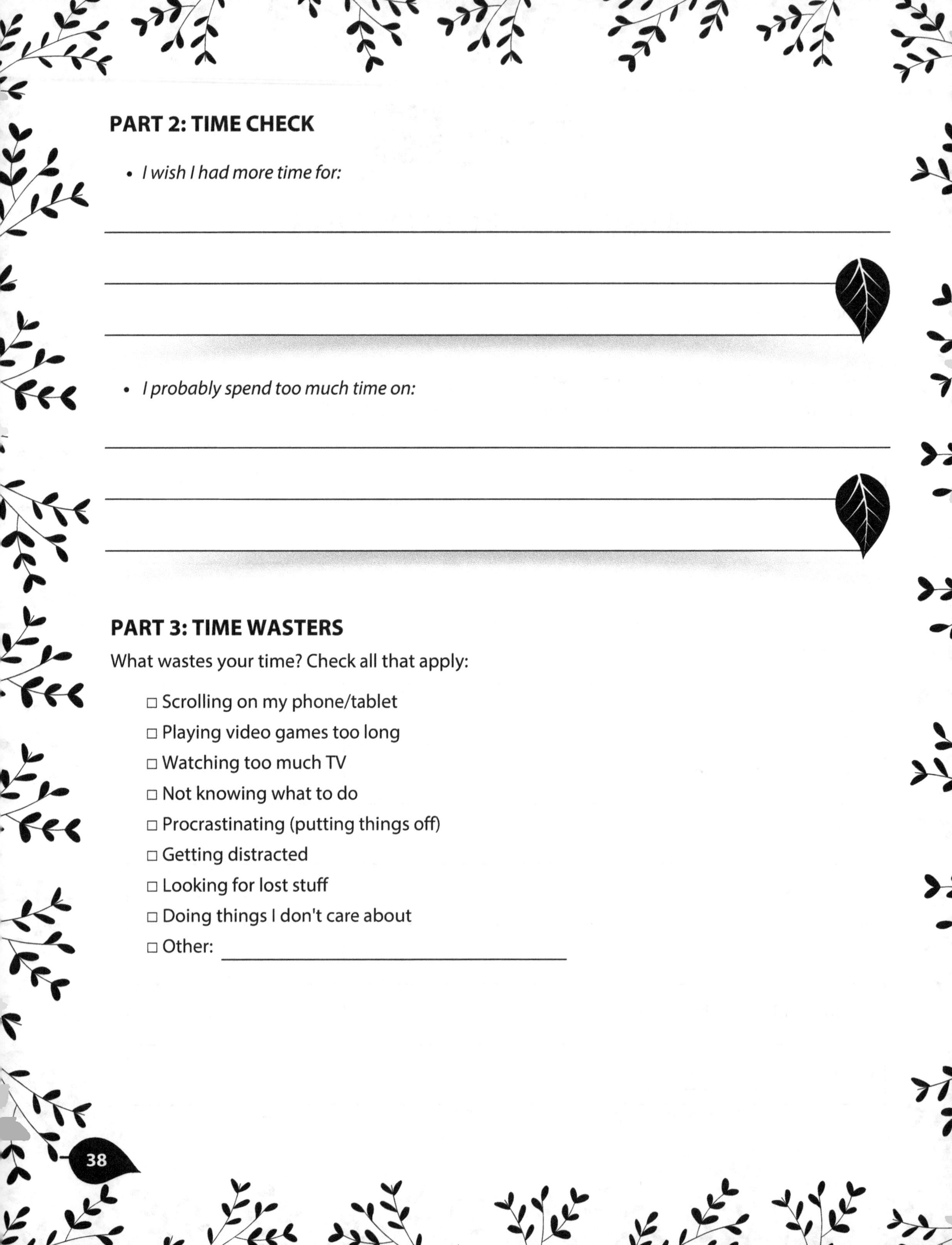

PART 2: TIME CHECK

- *I wish I had more time for:*

____

____

____

- *I probably spend too much time on:*

____

____

____

PART 3: TIME WASTERS

What wastes your time? Check all that apply:

☐ Scrolling on my phone/tablet

☐ Playing video games too long

☐ Watching too much TV

☐ Not knowing what to do

☐ Procrastinating (putting things off)

☐ Getting distracted

☐ Looking for lost stuff

☐ Doing things I don't care about

☐ Other: _______________________________

PART 4: ONE-WEEK TIME EXPERIMENT

- *This week, I'm going to try:*

____

____

____

____

(<u>Example</u>: *"Limit video games to 30 minutes on school nights" or "Do homework right after school instead of waiting")*

PART 5: MY IDEAL SPRING DAY

- *If I could spend my time exactly how I wanted, my perfect spring day would include:*

____

____

____

____

____

Time Tip:

You can't make more hours in the day, but you CAN choose how to use the hours you have!

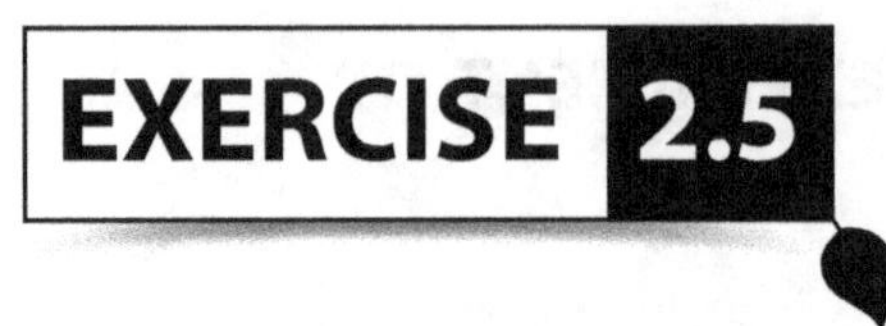

MY CALM-DOWN TOOLBOX

Everyone needs ways to calm down when they're upset, angry, worried, or stressed. Let's build YOUR toolbox!

PART 1: WHAT HELPS ME CALM DOWN?

Check all the things that help you feel better when you're upset:

MOVE YOUR BODY:

- □ Run or walk
- □ Dance
- □ Jump on trampoline
- □ Ride bike
- □ Play outside
- □ Stretch
- □ Sports

USE YOUR SENSES:

- □ Listen to music
- □ Take a shower
- □ Hug stuffed animal/pet
- □ Drink cold water
- □ Smell something nice
- □ Use fidget toy

BE CREATIVE:

- □ Draw or color
- □ Build something
- □ Play with clay
- □ Write in journal
- □ Play music

CALM YOUR MIND:

- □ Deep breathing
- □ Count to 10
- □ Think happy thoughts
- □ Look at pictures
- □ Read a book
- □ Watch funny videos

TALK IT OUT:

- □ Tell parent
- □ Call friend
- □ Talk to pet
- □ Write it down
- □ Tell teacher/counselor

PART 2: MY TOP 5 CALM-DOWN TOOLS

1. ____

2. ____

3. ____

4. ____

5. ____

PART 3: MATCHING TOOLS TO FEELINGS

Different feelings need different tools!

When I Feel...	I Can Try...
Angry or frustrated	<u>Example:</u> Run outside, punch a pillow, deep breaths
Worried or scared	
Sad or lonely	
Hyper or can't sit still	
Overwhelmed or stressed	

PART 4: QUICK CALM-DOWN: DEEP BREATHING

Try this RIGHT NOW!

The 5-Finger Breath:

1. Hold up one hand
2. Use your other pointer finger to trace your hand
3. Breathe IN as you trace up each finger
4. Breathe OUT as you trace down
5. Do all 5 fingers

How do you feel after doing this? ___________________________________

PART 5: MY CALM-DOWN PLAN

When I start to feel upset, my plan is:

- **Step 1:** Notice I'm getting upset
- **Step 2:** _______________________________________
- **Step 3:** _______________________________________
- **Step 4:** _______________________________________
- **Step 5:** _______________________________________

Remember:

The best time to use these tools is BEFORE you're super upset. Try to catch your feelings when they're still small!

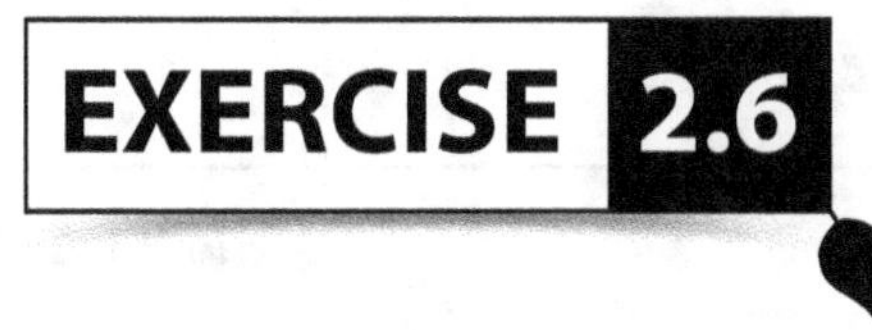

SLEEP, ENERGY, AND FEELING GOOD

How you sleep affects how you feel! Let's make sure you're getting what you need.

PART 1: SLEEP CHECK

Question	Your Answer
What time do you usually go to bed on school nights?	
What time do you wake up?	
About how many hours of sleep is that?	
Do you feel rested when you wake up?	
Do you have trouble falling asleep?	
Do you wake up during the night?	

Kids your age need: 9-12 hours of sleep!

PART 2: WHAT GETS IN THE WAY OF SLEEP?

Check what makes it hard for you to sleep:

□ Screen time before bed   □ Too much noise

□ Worrying or thinking too much   □ Uncomfortable bed   □ Scared of dark

□ Not tired yet   □ Nightmares   □ Have to use bathroom

□ Too hot or too cold   □ Other: ________________________

PART 3: BETTER SLEEP PLAN

Sleep Strategy	How I'll Do This
Bedtime routine	<u>Example:</u> Bath, brush teeth, read 15 min, lights out by 9pm
No screens before bed	
Comfortable room	
Calming down	
Bedtime	

PART 4: ENERGY LEVELS

Time of Day	My Energy (😴 Low / 😐 Medium / 😊 High)
Morning	
Afternoon	
After school	
Evening	

PART 5: SPRING ENERGY BOOST

- *One thing I can do this spring to have more energy:*

____

____

____

Sleep Tip: Try going to bed at the same time every night. Your body likes routines!

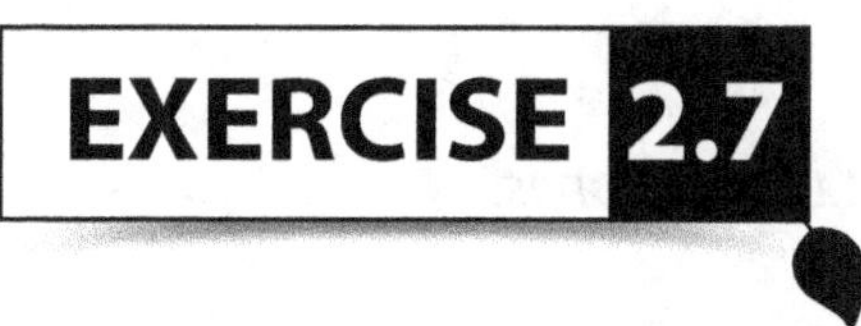

MY HEALTHY HABITS TRACKER

Healthy habits help you feel your best! Let's track what you're doing well and what you want to improve.

PART 1: CURRENT HABITS CHECK

How often do you do these healthy things? Mark each one:

Healthy Habit	Every Day	Sometimes	Rarely
Get enough sleep			
Eat breakfast			
Eat fruits/veggies			
Drink water			
Move my body/exercise			
Play outside			
Wash hands			
Brush teeth 2x day			
Limit screen time			
Spend time with people I like			

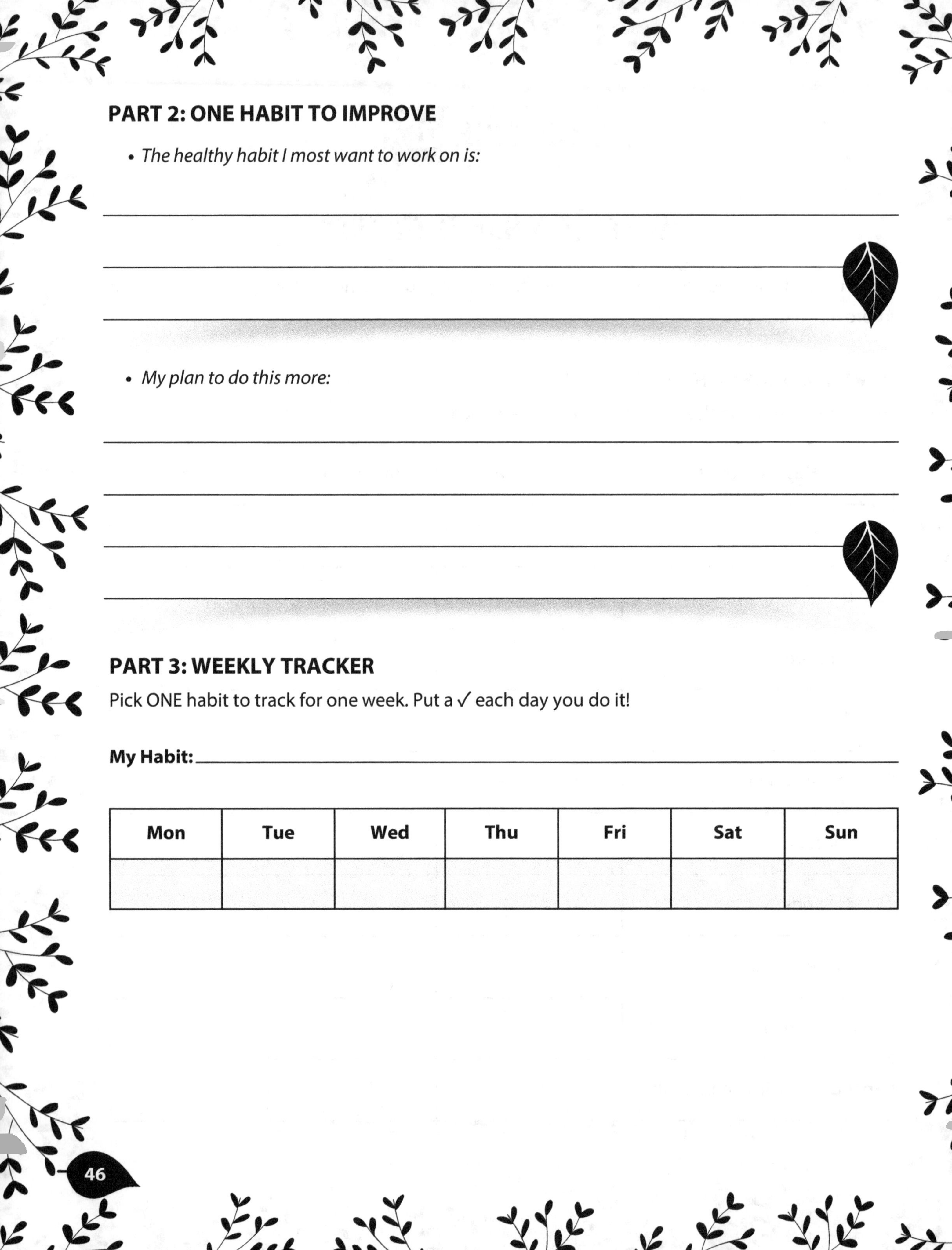

PART 2: ONE HABIT TO IMPROVE

- *The healthy habit I most want to work on is:*

____

____

____

- *My plan to do this more:*

____

____

____

PART 3: WEEKLY TRACKER

Pick ONE habit to track for one week. Put a ✓ each day you do it!

My Habit: ____

Mon	Tue	Wed	Thu	Fri	Sat	Sun

PART 4: WHAT HELPS, WHAT DOESN'T

Makes Healthy Habits EASIER	Makes Healthy Habits HARDER
<u>Example:</u> Having a water bottle at my desk	<u>Example:</u> Having junk food in the house

PART 5: SPRING HEALTH GOAL

- *By the end of spring, I want to:*

____

____

____

____

____

Habit Tip:

It takes about 3 weeks to build a new habit. Stick with it even when it's hard!

END OF CHAPTER 2: SELF-MANAGEMENT

Awesome work! You now have tools to manage stress, reach goals, and take care of yourself!

What's one self-management skill you're excited to practice this spring?

____

____

____

____

Up Next: Chapter 3 - Social Awareness

Learn how to understand others, show kindness, and make the world better!

CHAPTER 3

SOCIAL AWARENESS

Understanding Others

What is Social Awareness?

Social awareness means understanding and caring about other people, their feelings, their situations, and their experiences. It's about looking beyond yourself and seeing what's going on with others.

When you have good social awareness, you can:

- Tell how someone else is feeling
- Understand that people are different from you
- Show empathy (care about others' feelings)

- Notice when someone needs help
- Appreciate different cultures and backgrounds
- Make the world a little bit better

Why Does This Matter?

The world isn't just about you (even though you're pretty awesome!). There are billions of other people, each with their own feelings, problems, and experiences.

Social awareness helps you:

- Be a better friend
- Get along with more people
- Help others who need it
- Learn from people who are different from you
- Make your school and community better places

What You'll Learn in This Chapter:

In this chapter, you'll practice:

- Seeing things from someone else's point of view
- Reading people's feelings
- Being grateful for people in your life
- Showing kindness
- Understanding that everyone's spring is different
- Making a positive difference

Remember:

Being socially aware doesn't mean you have to fix everyone's problems. It just means you notice, you care, and you try to help when you can.

Let's learn about others!

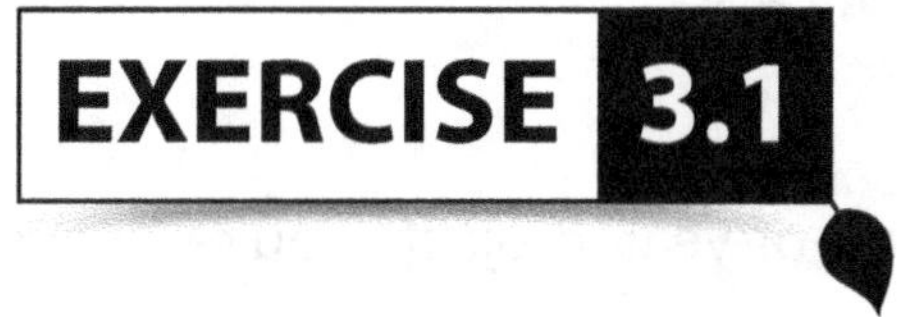

EXERCISE 3.1

SEEING THINGS SOMEONE ELSE'S WAY

Seeing someone else's point of view means imagining how THEY think and feel, not just how *YOU* do.

PART 1: SPRING SITUATION #1

The Situation:

It's a sunny spring day and your class has indoor recess because of a test. You're disappointed because you wanted to play outside. You notice your friend seems relieved.

- *Why might your friend be relieved about indoor recess?*

____

____

____

PART 2: SPRING SITUATION #2

The Situation:

Your friend group is planning a spring break trip to an amusement park. Everyone seems excited except one friend who keeps changing the subject.

- *What might be going on with that friend? Why might they not be excited?*

____

____

____

PART 3: SPRING SITUATION #3

The Situation:

Your teacher assigns a big end-of-year project. You're excited because you love the topic. Another student groans and looks upset.

- *Why might that student feel differently than you?*

____

____

____

____

PART 4: REAL LIFE PRACTICE

- *Think of a time when someone saw things differently than you. What was their point of view?*

____

____

____

PART 5: THE PERSPECTIVE CHALLENGE

- *This week, try asking someone: "How do you feel about that?" or "What do you think?" Write what you learned:*

____

____

____

Remember:

Just because someone sees things differently doesn't mean they're wrong. We all have different experiences!

EXERCISE 3.2

READING FACES AND FEELINGS

People's faces and bodies tell you a lot about how they're feeling—if you know what to look for!

PART 1: FEELING FACES

Match each face to the feeling: (Draw a line from the face to the feeling)

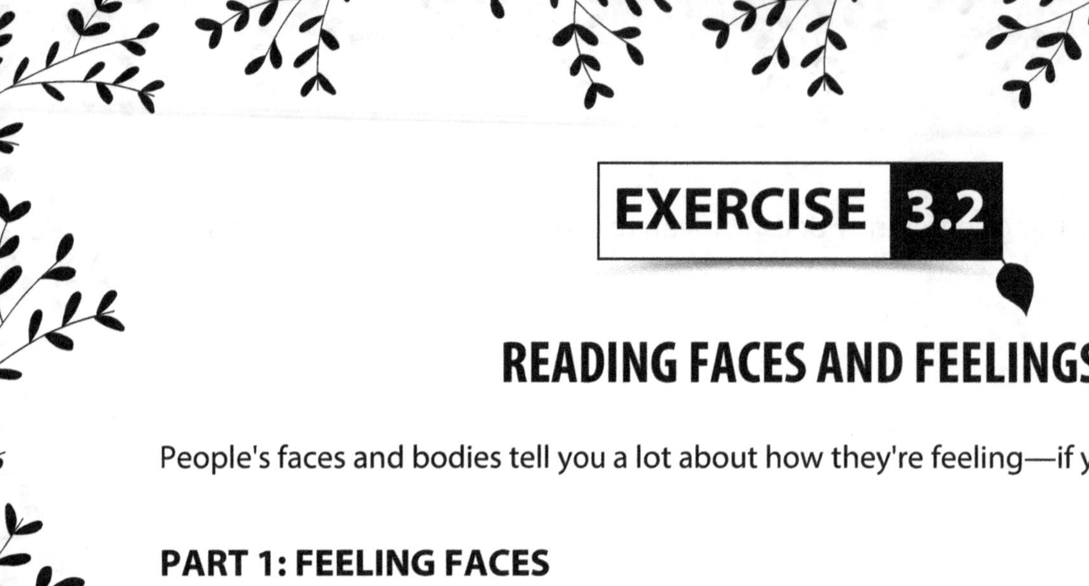

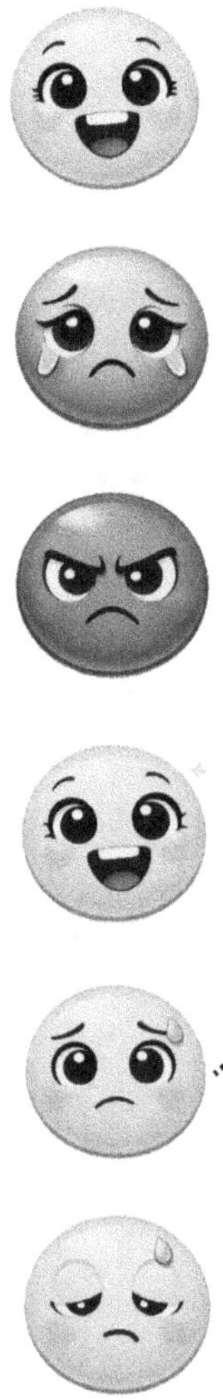

Worried

Happy

Sad

Bored

Excited

Angry

PART 2: BODY LANGUAGE

What do these body signals mean?

Body Signal	Might Mean...
Arms crossed, looking away	<u>Example:</u> Upset, closed off, don't want to talk
Bouncing, big smile	
Slouched, head down	
Hands on hips, frowning	
Fidgeting, looking around	
Relaxed, leaning forward	

PART 3: MIXED SIGNALS

Sometimes people's words don't match their feelings!

Situation: Your friend says *"I'm fine"* but they're looking down and speaking quietly.

- *What do you think they're REALLY feeling?*

____

____ 

____

- *What could you do or say?*

____

____ 

____

PART 4: PRACTICE IN REAL LIFE

Person	What I Noticed (face, body, voice)	What They Might Be Feeling
<u>Example:</u> My mom	Tired eyes, slow talking, sighing	Exhausted, stressed

PART 5: WHEN I'M NOT SURE

If I can't tell how someone is feeling, I can:

<u>Example:</u> *Ask them, "Are you okay?" or "How are you feeling?"*

____

____

____

____

Face-Reading Tip:

The best way to know how someone feels is to ASK them, not just guess!

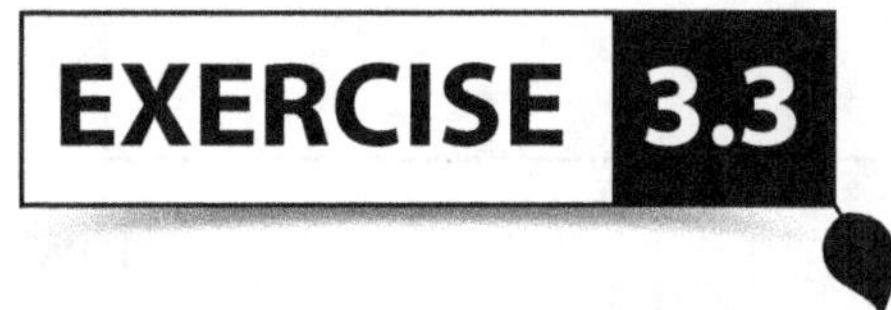

EXERCISE 3.3

PEOPLE WHO HELP ME

Let's think about all the people in your community who make your life better!

PART 1: MY COMMUNITY MAP

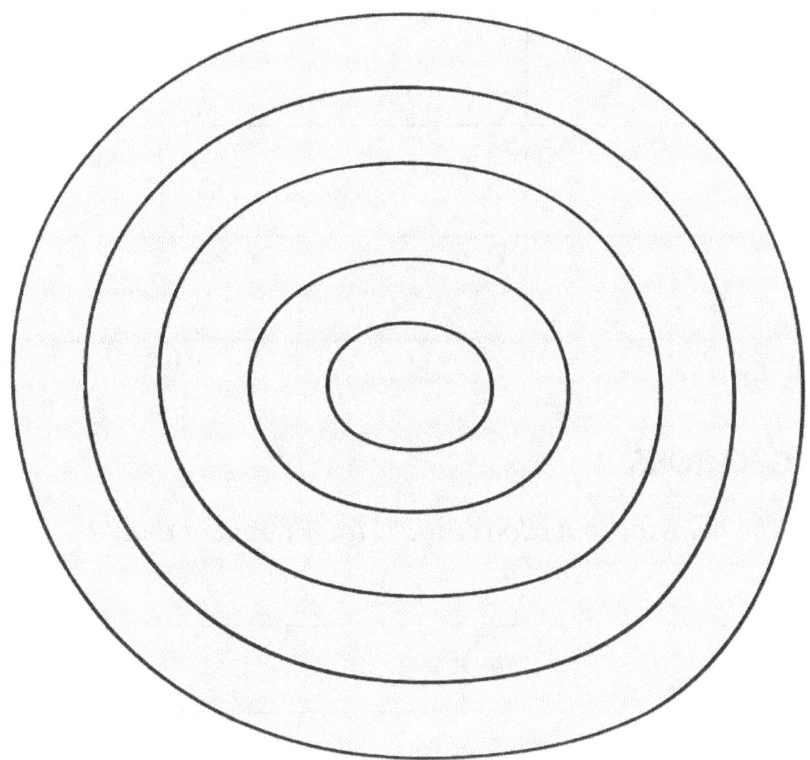

Draw or write people in each circle:

- **Center Circle:** You!
- **Circle 1:** Family (people you live with)
- **Circle 2:** Extended family & close friends
- **Circle 3:** School (teachers, friends, staff)
- **Circle 4:** Community (neighbors, coaches, store workers, etc.)

PART 2: THANK YOU LIST

Person	How They Help Me
<u>Example:</u> School bus driver	Gets me to school safely every day

PART 3: UNSUNG HEROES

- *Who's someone who helps me that I don't usually think about or thank?*

____

____

____

____

PART 4: HOW I HELP MY COMMUNITY

Place/Group	How I Help
<u>Example:</u> My family	Help with dishes, play with little brother

PART 5: SPRING COMMUNITY GOAL

- *One way I want to help my community this spring:*

____

____

____

____

Community Fact:

Communities work best when everyone helps each other!

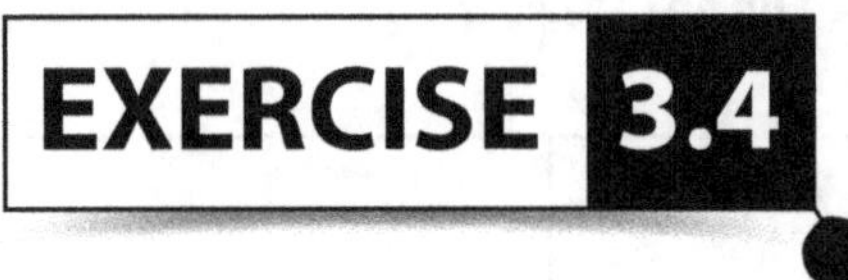

THANK YOU NOTES

Gratitude means being thankful. Let's practice saying thank you to people who matter!

PART 1: WHO TO THANK

List people you're grateful for:

Person	What I'm Thankful For
<u>Example:</u> My best friend	Always makes me laugh and includes me

PART 2: WRITE A THANK YOU NOTE

- *Pick someone from your list and write them a real thank you note!*

Dear_____________________,

I want to thank you for ____

You make me feel ____

Thank you for being ____

From,____ .

PART 3: DELIVERY PLAN

- *How will you give this thank you note to them?*

____

____

____

PART 4: SPRING GRATITUDE CHALLENGE

- *This spring, I commit to thanking _______ people in meaningful ways.*
- *Who and how:*

____

____

____

Gratitude Tip:

When you say thank you, be specific! Instead of just *"thanks,"* say *"Thank you for helping me with my homework. I really appreciate it!"*

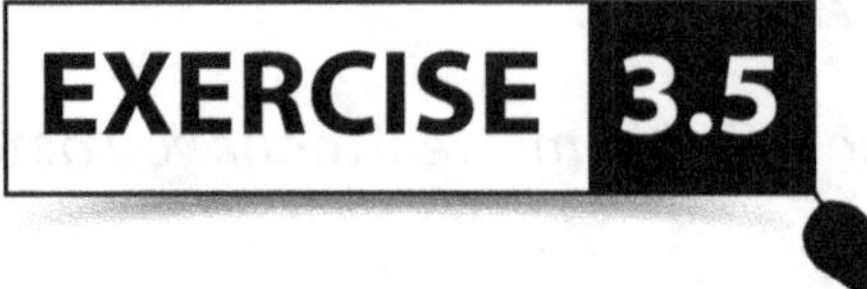

NOTICING WHEN SOMEONE NEEDS HELP

Part of caring about others is noticing when they might need help—even if they don't ask!

PART 1: SIGNS SOMEONE MIGHT NEED HELP

Check signs you've noticed in people:

☐ Looks sad or down

☐ Sitting alone

☐ Not talking as much

☐ Seems tired

☐ Getting mad easily

☐ Not doing homework

☐ Missing school a lot

☐ Looks worried

☐ Stopped doing things they used to like

☐ Giving things away

☐ Talking about feeling hopeless

☐ Has bruises or seems scared

If you notice serious signs (like the last two), tell a trusted adult immediately!

PART 2: DIFFERENT KINDS OF NEEDS

Type of Need	How I Could Help
Emotional (sad, upset, lonely)	<u>Example:</u> Sit with them, ask if they're okay, be a friend
School (struggling with work)	
Social (left out, no friends)	
Physical (hurt, sick, hungry)	

PART 3: WHEN I NOTICE...

- *I notice someone might need help when:*

____

____

____

PART 4: HOW TO OFFER HELP

You can say:

- *"Are you okay?"*
- *"Do you want to talk?"*
- *"Can I help you with that?"*
- *"Want to sit with me?"*
- *"I'm here if you need anything."*

- *If I notice someone needs help but I'm not sure what to do, I can:*

____

____

____

PART 5: SPRING HELPING GOAL

- *This spring, I will try to notice when people need help and:*

____

____

____

Important:

Sometimes the best help is telling a trusted adult. You don't have to fix everything yourself!

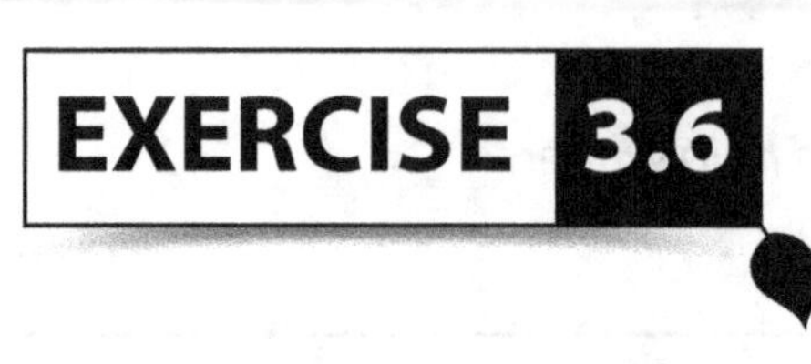

KINDNESS CHALLENGE

Being kind makes *YOU* feel good and makes others feel good too! Let's spread some kindness this spring.

PART 1: KINDNESS BRAINSTORM

- How many acts of kindness can you think of?

____

____

____

PART 2: RANDOM ACTS OF KINDNESS

Try to do ONE kind thing each day for a week!

Day	Kind Thing I Did	How It Felt
Monday		
Tuesday		
Wednesday		
Thursday		
Friday		
Saturday		
Sunday		

PART 3: KINDNESS IN DIFFERENT PLACES

Place	Kind Thing I Can Do
At home	<u>Example:</u> Make my bed without being asked
At school	
With friends	
In my community	

PART 4: SECRET KINDNESS

- *Do something kind WITHOUT anyone knowing it was you! What will you do?*

____

____

____

____

PART 5: KINDNESS REFLECTION

- *After being extra kind this week, what did you notice? How did it feel?*

____

____

____

Kindness Fact:

Being kind actually makes *YOU* happier too! Scientists have proven it!

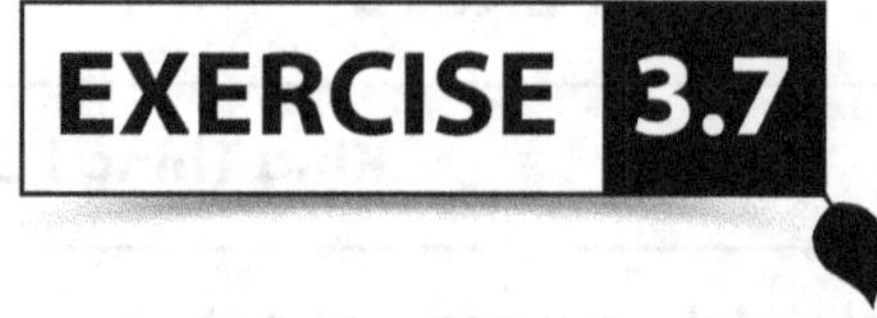

BEING A GOOD FRIEND TO EVERYONE

Being socially aware means trying to include everyone and make people feel welcome!

PART 1: WHO GETS LEFT OUT?

- *At my school, I notice these kids sometimes get left out: (You don't have to name names—just describe types of kids)*

____

____

____

____

PART 2: HOW IT FEELS

- *Have you ever been left out? How did it feel?*

____

____

____

PART 3: INCLUDING OTHERS

Situation	How I Can Include Someone
Someone sitting alone at lunch	<u>Example:</u> "Want to sit with us?"
Someone picked last for teams	
New kid in class	
Someone who seems shy	

PART 4: SPRING INCLUSION CHALLENGE

- *This spring, I will try to include people by:*

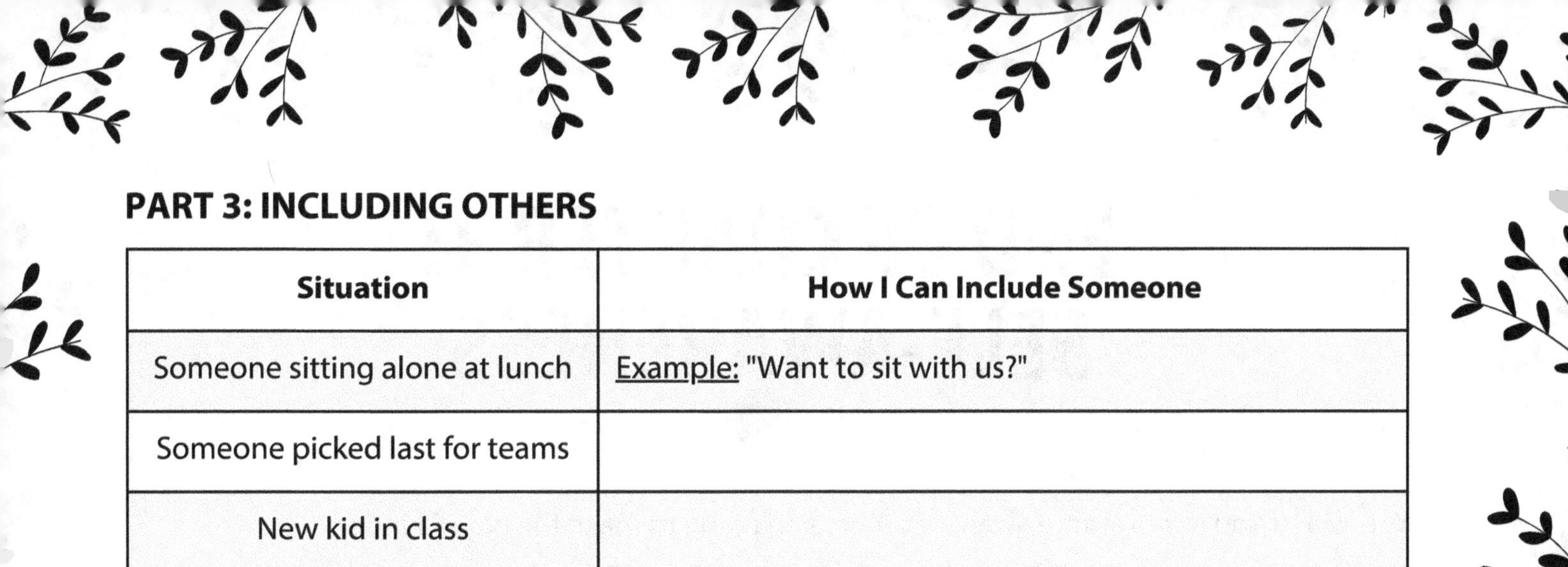

PART 5: STANDING UP FOR OTHERS

- *If I see someone being mean or leaving someone out, I can:*

Inclusion Reminder:

Everyone wants to feel like they belong. You have the power to help people feel that way!

END OF CHAPTER 3: SELF-AWARENESS

You did it! You're now more aware of others and ready to make the world kinder!

- *What's one way you'll show you care about others this spring?*

____

____

____

____

➥ Up Next: Chapter 4 - Relationship Skills

Learn how to be an awesome friend, solve problems, and get along with everyone!

CHAPTER 4

RELATIONSHIP SKILLS

Getting Along with Others

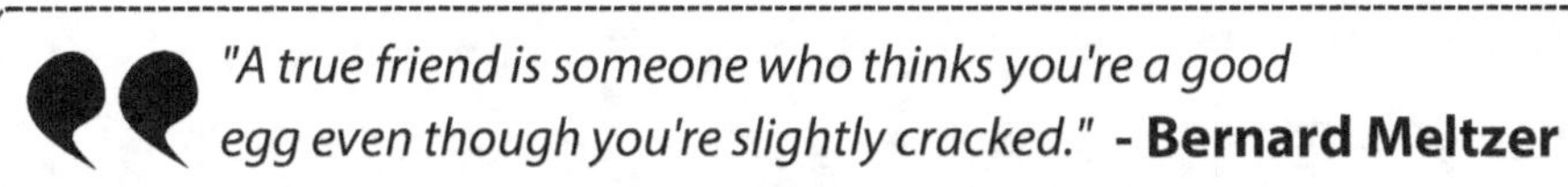

"A true friend is someone who thinks you're a good egg even though you're slightly cracked." **- Bernard Meltzer**

What Are Relationship Skills?

Relationship skills are the abilities you need to get along with people, making friends, keeping friends, working with others, communicating clearly, and solving problems when people don't agree.

When you have good relationship skills, you can:

- Make new friends and keep old ones
- Work well with others in groups

- Talk about your feelings without fighting
- Solve problems when friends disagree
- Know when to say yes and when to say no
- Get along with family members
- Stand up for yourself in kind ways

Why Does This Matter?

Humans need other humans! We're meant to have friends, family, and communities. But getting along with people isn't always easy, it takes practice!

Good relationship skills help you:
- Have better friendships
- Feel less lonely
- Get through tough times with help from others
- Work better in groups at school
- Have more fun with friends
- Feel more confident in social situations

What You'll Learn in This Chapter:

In this chapter, you'll practice:
- Mapping out your friendships
- Communicating clearly
- Solving friend problems
- Setting boundaries
- Making new friends
- Working well in groups
- Fixing friendships that are broken

Remember:

Even the best friendships have problems sometimes. That's normal! What matters is knowing how to work through them.

Let's build better relationships!

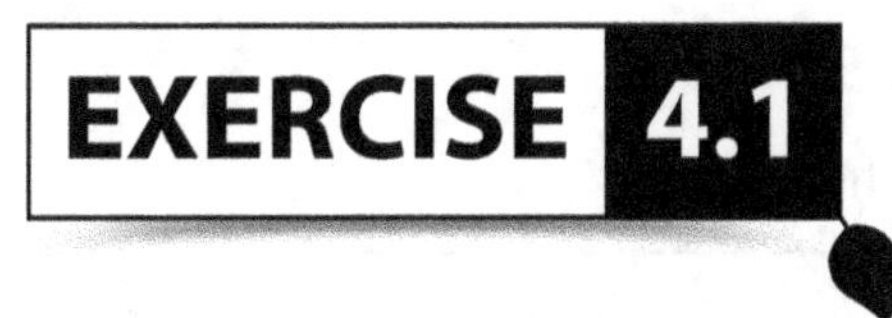

MY FRIEND MAP

Let's look at your friendships and see what's working and what's not!

PART 1: FRIENDSHIP CIRCLES

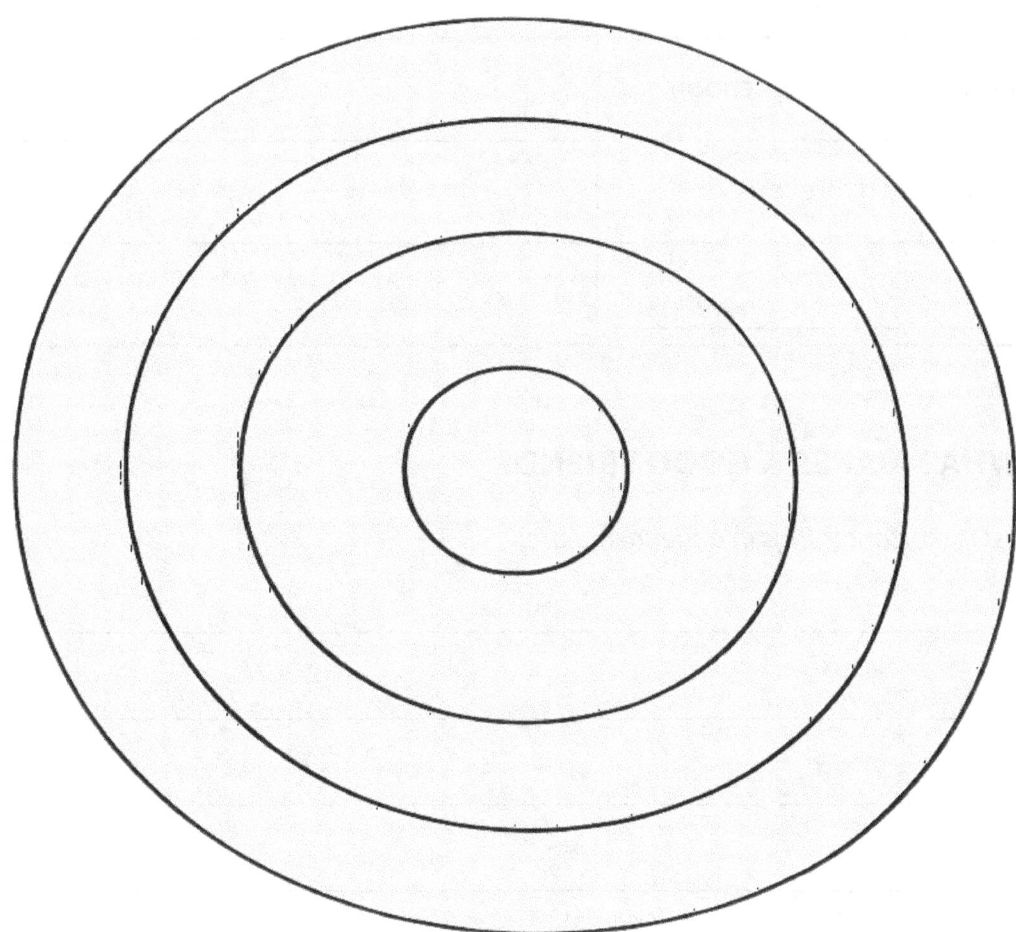

Put yourself in the center circle. Then put friends in the other circles:

- **Ring 1 (Closest):** Your very best friends
- **Ring 2 (Close):** Good friends you like spending time with
- **Ring 3 (Friends):** People you're friendly with but not super close to

PART 2: FRIENDSHIP TYPES

Everyone has different types of friends!

Type of Friend	Who This Is For Me
Best friend (tell everything to)	
Fun friend (always makes me laugh)	
Activity friend (play sports/games with)	
School friend (mostly see at school)	
Family friend (known forever)	
Other: ______________________________	

PART 3: WHAT MAKES A GOOD FRIEND?

- *The most important things in a friendship are:*

____

____

____

____

____

PART 4: FRIENDSHIP CHECK

- Pick one important friendship:

Question	Answer
What do I like about this friendship?	
What do I give to this friendship?	
What does my friend give?	
Is it balanced or one-sided?	
Do I feel good after spending time with them?	

PART 5: SPRING FRIENDSHIP GOAL

- *This spring, I want to:*

(<u>Examples:</u> Make a new friend, spend more time with a current friend, fix a friendship that's struggling)

____

____

____

____

Friendship Fact:

Quality matters more than quantity. It's better to have a few good friends than lots of not-so-great ones!

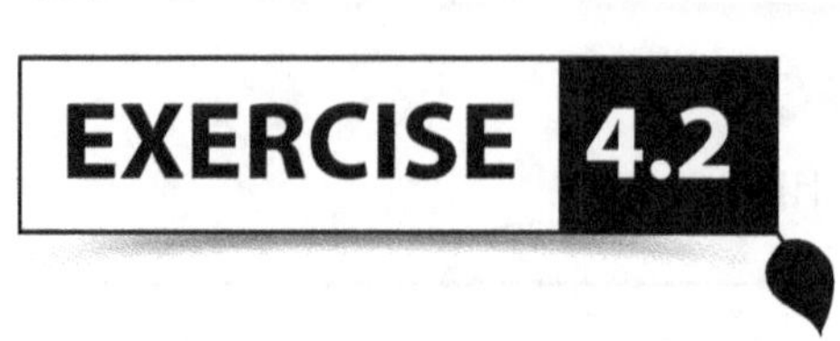

HOW I TALK TO OTHERS

How you communicate affects your relationships! Let's figure out your style.

PART 1: COMMUNICATION QUIZ

- **Your friend borrowed your favorite game and returned it broken. What do you do?**

  A) Don't say anything. It's just a game.

  B) Give them the silent treatment so they know you're mad.

  C) Yell at them: "You broke my game! You're so careless!"

  D) Say calmly: "Hey, my game got broken. Can we figure out what happened?"

- **Your friend keeps interrupting you when you're trying to tell a story. What do you do?**

  A) Stop talking and let them take over.

  B) Interrupt them back to show how it feels.

  C) Say rudely: "Can you PLEASE let me talk?!"

  D) Say: "Hold on, I want to finish my story first."

- **You don't want to go to a party your friends are going to. What do you do?**

  A) Go even though you don't want to.

  B) Say "whatever" in an annoyed voice.

  C) Say: "That party sounds stupid anyway."

  D) Say: "That's not really my thing, but have fun!"

SCORING:

Mostly A's = Passive - You avoid saying what you want

Mostly B's = Passive-Aggressive - You show you're upset indirectly

Mostly C's = Aggressive - You say what you want but in a mean way

Mostly D's = Assertive - You say what you want respectfully

GOAL:

Assertive is best! It means you speak up for yourself while being kind to others.

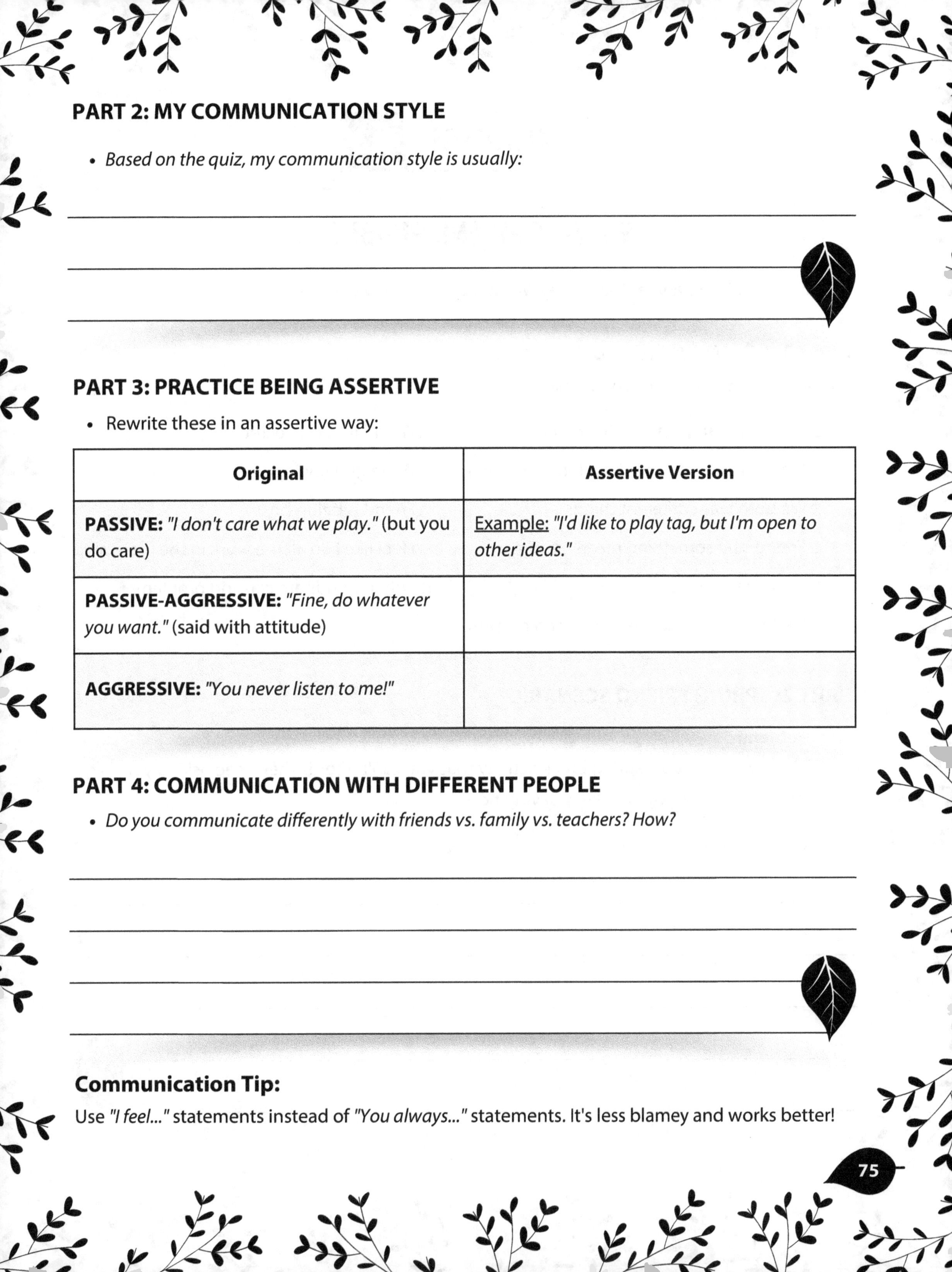

PART 2: MY COMMUNICATION STYLE

- *Based on the quiz, my communication style is usually:*

____

____

____

PART 3: PRACTICE BEING ASSERTIVE

- Rewrite these in an assertive way:

Original	Assertive Version
PASSIVE: *"I don't care what we play."* (but you do care)	Example: *"I'd like to play tag, but I'm open to other ideas."*
PASSIVE-AGGRESSIVE: *"Fine, do whatever you want."* (said with attitude)	
AGGRESSIVE: *"You never listen to me!"*	

PART 4: COMMUNICATION WITH DIFFERENT PEOPLE

- *Do you communicate differently with friends vs. family vs. teachers? How?*

____

____

____

Communication Tip:

Use *"I feel..."* statements instead of *"You always..."* statements. It's less blamey and works better!

EXERCISE 4.3

SOLVING FRIEND PROBLEMS

Friends don't always agree. That's okay! What matters is how you handle it.

PART 1: COMMON FRIEND PROBLEMS

Check any friend problems you've had:

- ☐ Friend is mad at me and won't talk
- ☐ I'm mad at friend and they don't know why
- ☐ We both want different things
- ☐ Friend said something mean
- ☐ Friend left me out
- ☐ I left friend out (accidentally or on purpose)

- ☐ Friend told my secret
- ☐ We're growing apart
- ☐ Friend is being bossy
- ☐ I feel like I do all the work in the friendship
- ☐ Other friends are causing problems

PART 2: SPRING FRIEND SCENARIO

The Problem:

Your friend wants to do a spring break activity that you can't afford. They keep asking you to go and don't understand why you keep saying no.

- *How would you handle this?*

____

____

____

____

____

PART 3: SPRING FRIEND SCENARIO

The Problem:
You and your friend both want to be team captain for a spring sports team. Now things feel awkward between you.

- *How would you handle this?*

____

____

____

____

PART 4: PROBLEM-SOLVING STEPS

When you have a friend problem:

1. □ **Calm down first** - Don't try to solve it when you're super upset

2. □ **Talk to your friend** - Pick a private time

3. □ **Use "I feel" statements** - "I feel hurt when..."

4. □ **Listen to their side** - Really hear what they say

5. □ **Apologize if needed** - Even if you're also upset

6. □ **Find a solution together** - Both people should feel okay

7. □ **Move forward** - Don't hold grudges

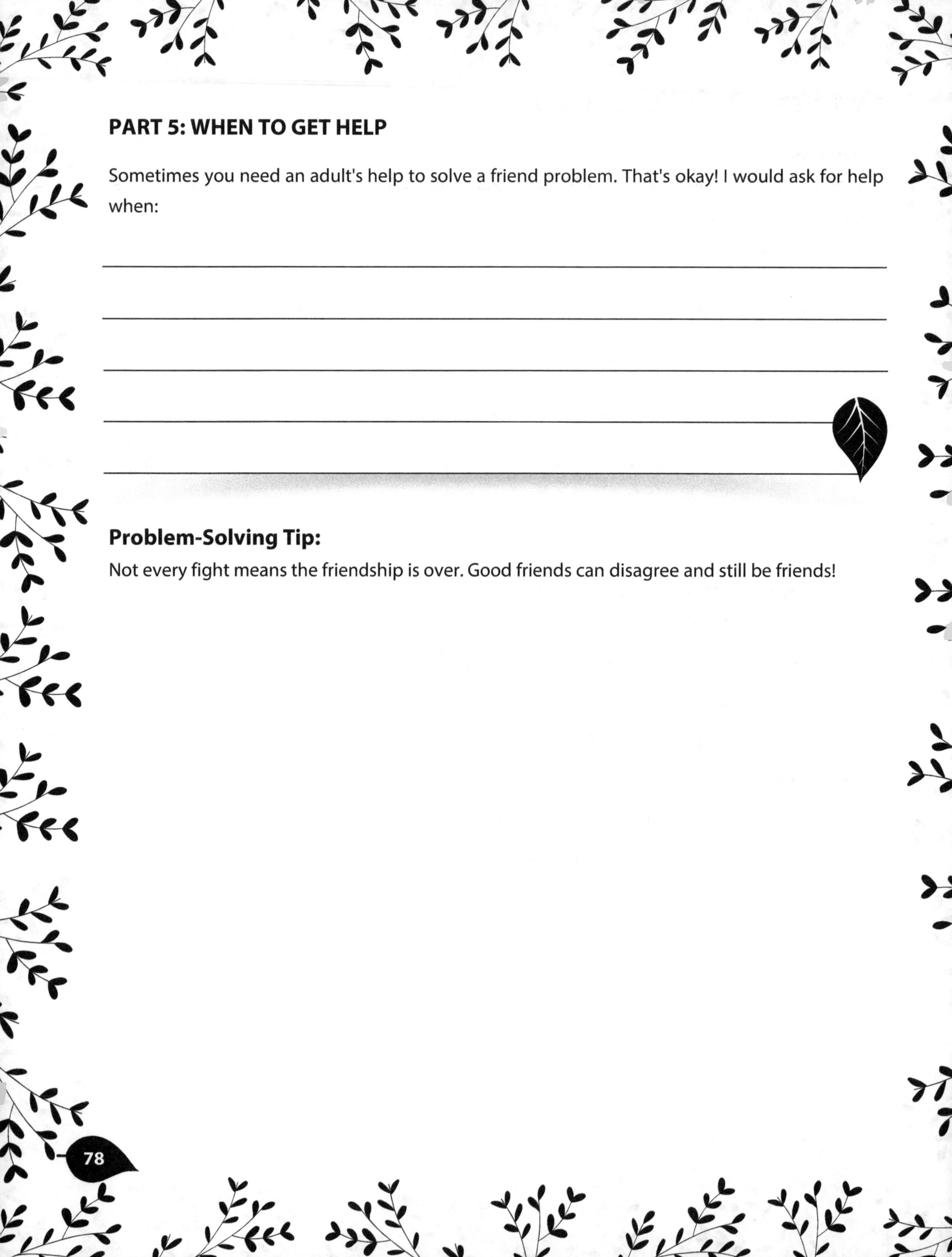

PART 5: WHEN TO GET HELP

Sometimes you need an adult's help to solve a friend problem. That's okay! I would ask for help when:

____

____

____

____

____

Problem-Solving Tip:

Not every fight means the friendship is over. Good friends can disagree and still be friends!

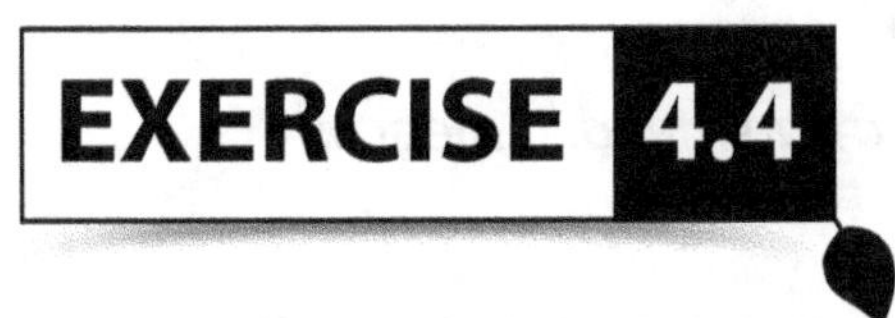

SAYING NO WHEN I NEED TO

Saying no can be hard, but sometimes you need to!

PART 1: WHEN TO SAY NO

It's okay to say no when:

☐ Something makes you uncomfortable

☐ You need alone time

☐ You're already too busy

☐ It goes against your values

☐ You don't want to

☐ Your gut says it's not safe

☐ You'd be breaking rules

☐ It would hurt someone

☐ You need to take care of yourself

PART 2: PRACTICE SAYING NO

Situation	How to Say No
Friend wants to copy your homework	<u>Example:</u> "I can help you understand it, but I can't let you copy."
Invited to a party but you're exhausted	
Friend wants you to be mean to someone	
Too many activities to do them all	

PART 3: "NO" ISN'T MEAN

- *Saying no doesn't make you a bad friend. It means:*

____

____

____

____

PART 4: WHEN FRIENDS DON'T ACCEPT MY "NO"

- *If I say no and someone keeps pushing me or makes me feel bad, I can:*

____

____

____

____

PART 5: SPRING "NO" PRACTICE

- *Something I might need to say no to this spring:*

____

____

____

____

"No" Tip:

You don't always have to explain. *"No thanks"* or *"That doesn't work for me"* is enough!

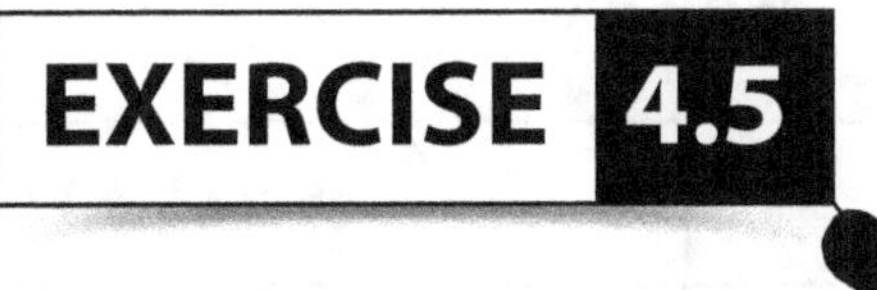

MAKING NEW FRIENDS

Want to make new friends this spring? Here's how!

PART 1: WHY MAKE NEW FRIENDS?

- I'd like to make new friends because:

____

____

____

____

____

PART 2: WHAT I'M LOOKING FOR

Quality	Why This Matters to Me
<u>Example:</u> Likes same activities	So we have fun things to do together

PART 3: WHERE TO MEET PEOPLE

Place/Activity	Will I Try This? (Yes/Maybe/No)
Join a spring sport or club	
Talk to someone new at lunch	
Go to a community event	
Say hi to kids in my neighborhood	
Ask to join a game at recess	

PART 4: CONVERSATION STARTERS

What can you say to start a conversation?

☐ "Cool [shirt/shoes/backpack]. Where'd you get it?"

☐ "Want to play?"

☐ "Can I sit here?"

☐ "Did you do the homework? It was so hard!"

☐ "What are you doing for spring break?"

☐ "Do you like [game/show/sport]?"

☐ "I'm [name]. What's your name?"

PART 5: FROM "HI" TO FRIEND

Steps to turn someone from acquaintance to friend:

1. Say hi and talk a few times

2. Find something in common

3. Ask if they want to hang out

4. Do something fun together

5. Stay in touch

6. Keep spending time together

PART 6: IF THEY SAY NO

- *If I try to make friends and it doesn't work out, I'll remember:*

____

____

____

____

____

Friend-Making Tip:

Not everyone will be your friend, and that's okay! Just keep being yourself and trying!

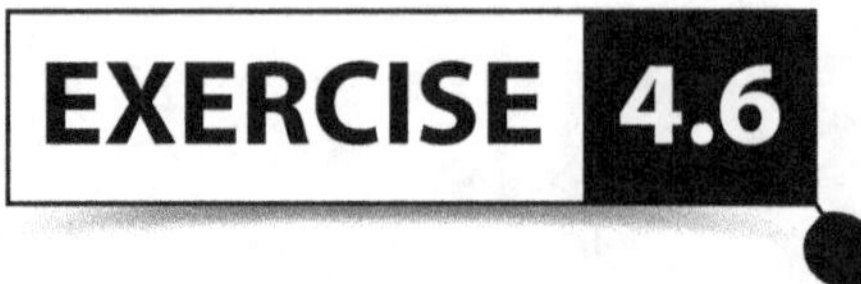

WORKING IN GROUPS

Group projects and team activities happen a lot in spring! Let's get better at working with others.

PART 1: MY GROUP WORK STYLE

How do you usually act in groups? Check all that apply:

☐ I like to be the leader

☐ I like hearing everyone's ideas

☐ I go along with what others want

☐ I have good ideas but don't always share them

☐ I get frustrated when people don't agree with me

☐ I let others do most of the work

☐ I work best alone

☐ I do most of the work

PART 4: WHEN FRIENDSHIPS CHANGE

Challenge	What I Can Do
Someone isn't doing their share	<u>Example:</u> "Hey, can you work on this part? We need everyone to help."
People keep interrupting	
We can't agree on what to do	
One person wants to control everything	

PART 3: BEING A GOOD GROUP MEMBER

In my next group project, I will:

□ Listen to others' ideas　　　　□ Help others if they're struggling

□ Share my own ideas　　　　　□ Speak up if something isn't fair

□ Do my fair share of work　　　□ Stay positive

□ Be nice even when I disagree

PART 4: DIFFERENT ROLES

Group Role	Am I Good at This?
Leader/organizer	
Idea person	
Worker (gets stuff done)	
Peacemaker (helps people get along)	
Encourager (keeps spirits up)	

PART 5: SPRING GROUP GOAL

- *In my next group project or team activity, I want to be better at:*

____

____

____

____

Group Work Tip:

Everyone has different strengths. A good group uses everyone's talents!

FIXING FRIENDSHIPS

Sometimes friendships get damaged. Here's how to repair them!

PART 1: FRIENDSHIP PROBLEMS

- *Is there a friendship that's not going well right now? What happened?*

PART 2: MY PART IN IT

Even if it wasn't all your fault, what was your part?

- *What I did (or didn't do):*

PART 3: WHAT I WANT

- *Do I want to fix this friendship? Why or why not?*

PART 4: MAKING AMENDS

If you want to fix it, you need to:

1. □ Admit what you did wrong

2. □ Say you're sorry (and mean it)

3. □ Listen to their feelings

4. □ Make a plan to do better

5. □ Give them time if they need it

6. □ Follow through on your promises

PART 5: WHAT TO SAY

- *Practice what you would say to your friend:*

____

____

____

____

PART 6: WHEN TO LET GO

- *Sometimes friendships can't be fixed, and that's okay. I'll know it's time to let go if:*

____

____

____

____

Fixing Friendships Tip:

A real apology includes: *"I'm sorry,"* what you did wrong, and how you'll do better. Not just *"Sorry you're mad."*

END OF CHAPTER 4: RELATIONSHIP SKILLS

Great job! You now have skills to build and maintain awesome friendships!

- *What's one relationship skill you want to practice this spring?*

____

____

____

____

____

➡ Up Next: Chapter 5 - Responsible Decision-Making

Learn how to make smart choices about spring activities, summer plans, and more!

RESPONSIBLE DECISION-MAKING

Making Good Choices

> 🗨🗨 *"Every choice you make has an end result."* **- Zig Ziglar**

What is Responsible Decision-Making?

Responsible decision-making means thinking before you act, considering consequences, and making choices that are good for you AND others. It's about making smart choices, even when they're hard!

When you're good at making decisions, you can:

- Think through options before choosing
- Consider how choices affect you and others

- Make choices based on what's right, not just what's easy
- Learn from mistakes
- Plan ahead for important stuff

Why Does This Matter?

You make hundreds of choices every day! Some are small (what to wear, what to eat) and some are bigger (how to spend your free time, how to treat others, what activities to join).

Good decision-making helps you:
- Avoid problems before they happen
- Feel proud of your choices
- Reach your goals
- Stay safe and healthy
- Get along better with others

What You'll Learn in This Chapter:

In this chapter, you'll practice:
- Using a framework for making decisions
- Evaluating opportunities
- Handling peer pressure
- Knowing right from wrong
- Planning your summer
- Taking care of your body and mind
- Creating your spring action plan

Remember:

Nobody makes perfect decisions all the time. The goal is to think things through and try your best!

Let's get better at making choices!

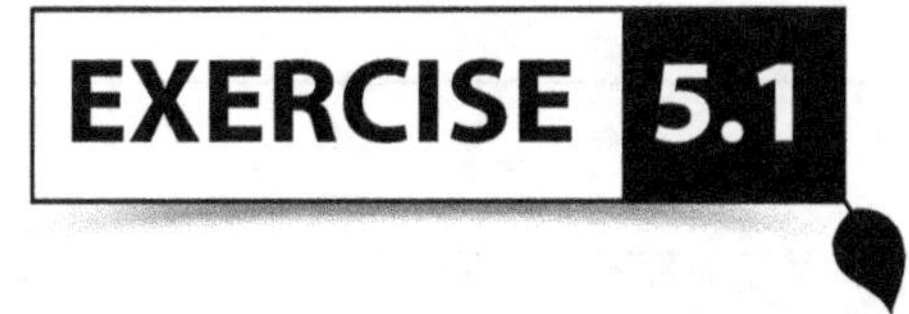

HOW TO MAKE GOOD DECISIONS

Having a system for making decisions helps you make better ones!

PART 1: THE THINK FRAMEWORK

When you have a decision to make, THINK:

T - Think about what you're deciding

H - How will this affect me and others?

I - Is this safe and right?

N - Note the options I have

K - Keep or choose the best option

PART 2: PRACTICE WITH A REAL DECISION

Think of a decision you need to make right now:

- *T - What am I deciding?*

____

____

____

____

- *H - How will this affect me and others?*

____

____

____

____

- *I - Is this safe and right?*

____

____

____

- *N - What are my options?*

Option	Pros and Cons
1	
2	
3	

- *K - My decision:*

____

____

____

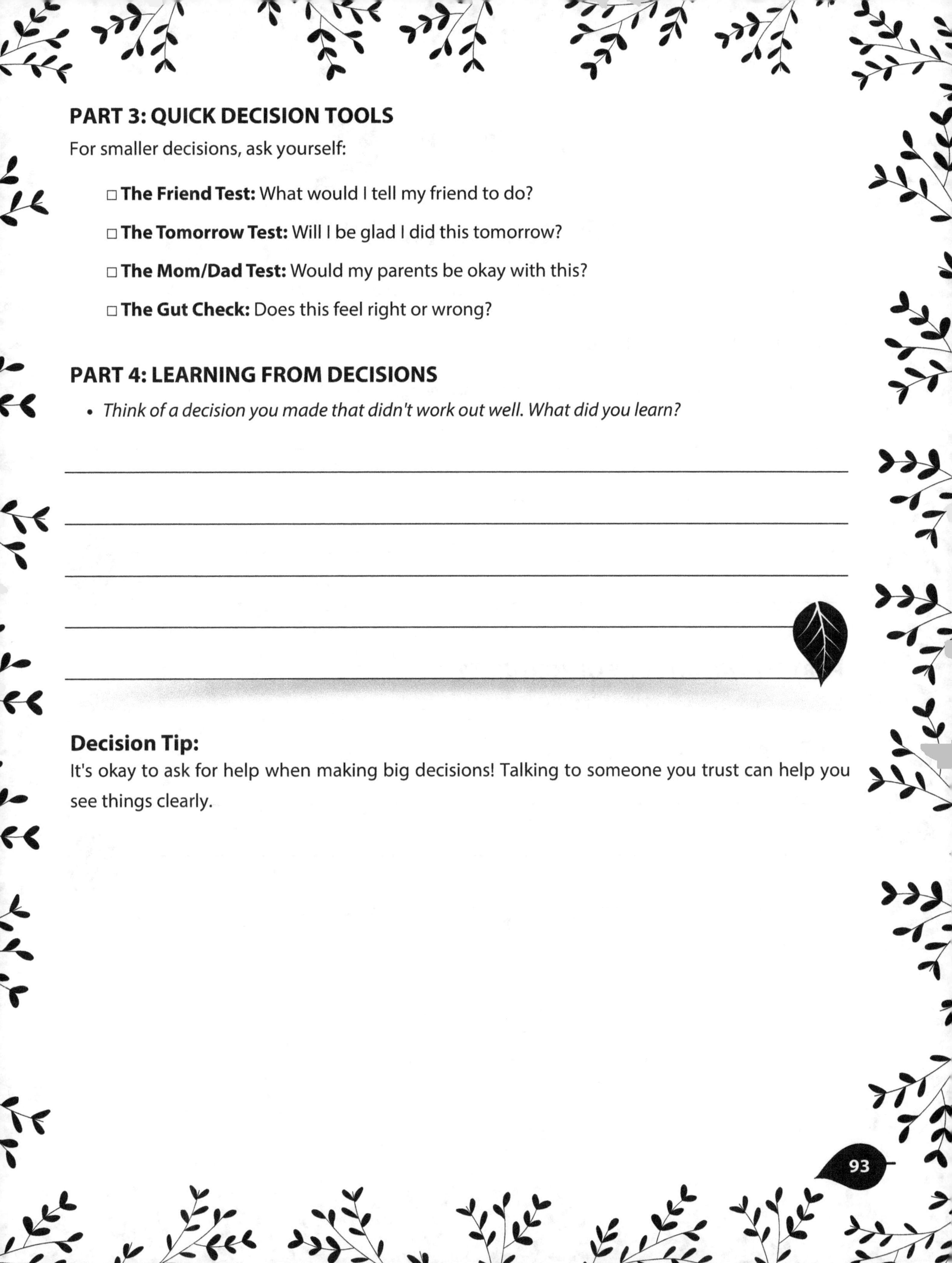

PART 3: QUICK DECISION TOOLS

For smaller decisions, ask yourself:

- ☐ **The Friend Test:** What would I tell my friend to do?

- ☐ **The Tomorrow Test:** Will I be glad I did this tomorrow?

- ☐ **The Mom/Dad Test:** Would my parents be okay with this?

- ☐ **The Gut Check:** Does this feel right or wrong?

PART 4: LEARNING FROM DECISIONS

- *Think of a decision you made that didn't work out well. What did you learn?*

____

____

____

____

Decision Tip:

It's okay to ask for help when making big decisions! Talking to someone you trust can help you see things clearly.

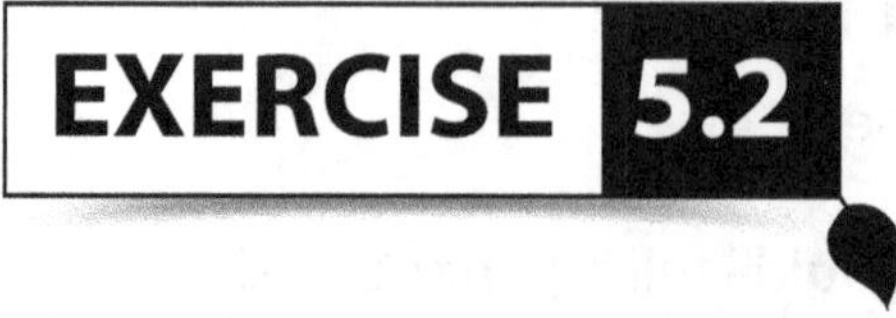

EXERCISE 5.2

SHOULD I DO THIS OR NOT?

Spring brings lots of opportunities! Let's figure out which ones to say yes to.

PART 1: SPRING OPPORTUNITIES

- *What opportunities or choices do you have this spring?*

____

____

____ 

____

PART 2: EVALUATE ONE OPPORTUNITY

Pick one from above and think it through:

- *The opportunity is:*

____

____

SMART CHECK:

Question	Answer
Does this match what I care about?	
Will I have enough time?	
Can I afford it (or can my family)?	
Will this help me reach my goals?	
Do I actually WANT to do this?	

GOOD THINGS ABOUT THIS:

____

____

____

CHALLENGING THINGS ABOUT THIS:

____

____

____

PART 3: THE YES/NO DECISION

- *Based on everything above, my decision is:*

____

____

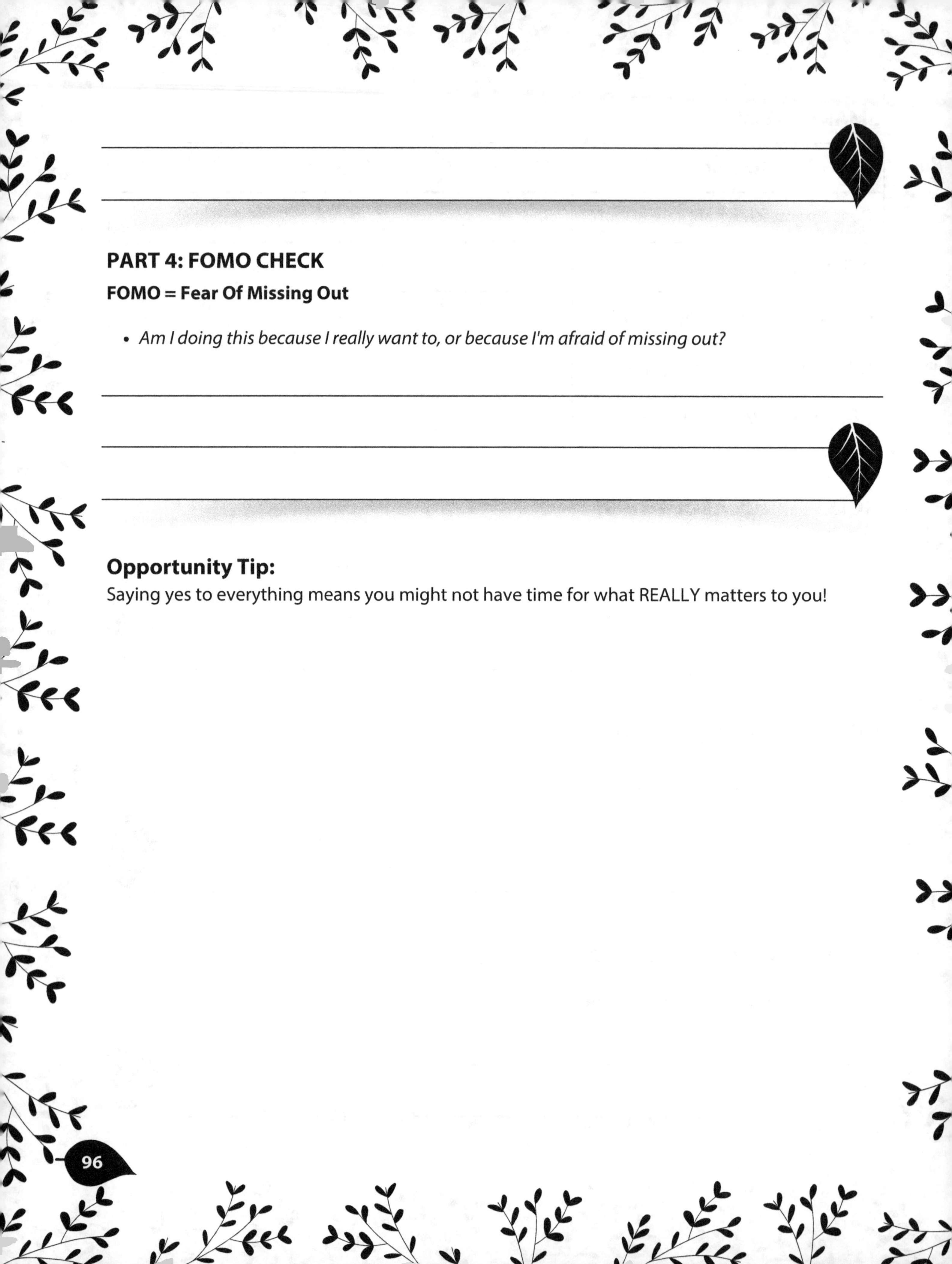# PART 4: FOMO CHECK

FOMO = Fear Of Missing Out

- *Am I doing this because I really want to, or because I'm afraid of missing out?*

Opportunity Tip:

Saying yes to everything means you might not have time for what REALLY matters to you!

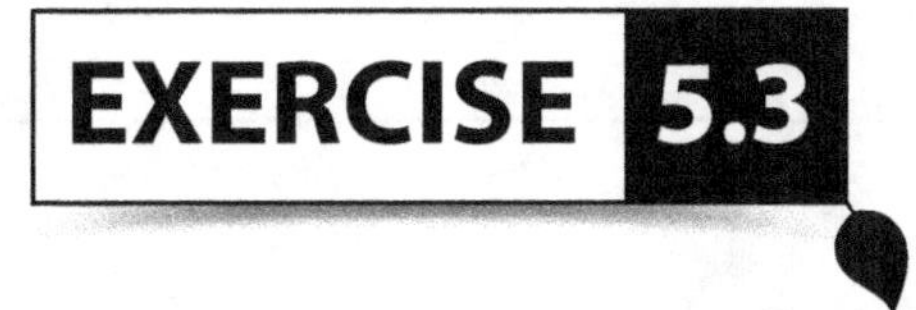

WHEN FRIENDS WANT ME TO DO SOMETHING

Peer pressure is when friends try to get you to do something, even if you don't want to. Let's prepare for it!

PART 1: TYPES OF PEER PRESSURE

I've felt peer pressure to:

☐ Do something I didn't want to do

☐ Be mean to someone

☐ Break rules

☐ Try something dangerous

☐ Go somewhere I shouldn't

☐ Lie or cheat

☐ Do something my parents wouldn't like

☐ Buy something I can't afford

☐ Join in making fun of someone

☐ Keep a secret I shouldn't

PART 2: SPRING PRESSURE SCENARIOS

Scenario 1:

Your friends want to sneak out to a spring festival that your parents said you can't go to.

- *What would you do?*

____

____

Scenario 2:

Everyone's posting spring break photos and you feel pressured to make YOUR spring break look as exciting as theirs.

- *What would you do?*

Scenario 3:

Your friends dare you to climb over a fence to get into a pool that's closed.

- *What would you do?*

PART 3: WAYS TO SAY NO

Strategy	What to Say
Direct	*"No thanks."*
Give a reason	
Suggest something else	
Blame someone else	
Just leave	
Get help from adult	

PART 4: REAL FRIENDS DON'T PRESSURE

- *Real friends will respect when I say no because:*

____

____

____

____

____

Peer Pressure Tip:
If someone makes you feel bad for saying no, they're not being a good friend!

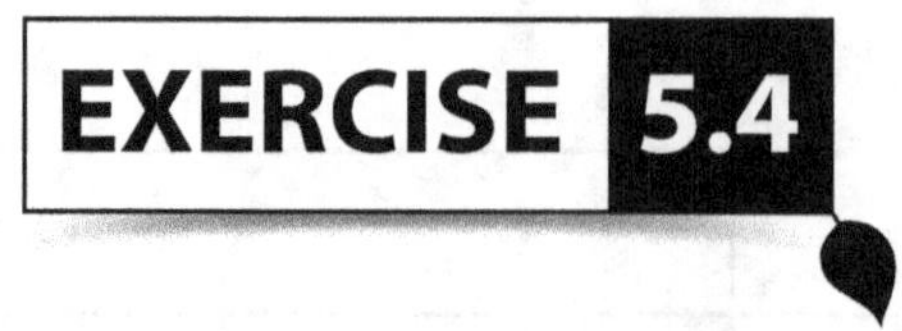

RIGHT, WRONG, OR IN-BETWEEN?

Sometimes it's easy to know what's right and wrong. Sometimes it's not! Let's practice.

PART 1: CLEAR RIGHT AND WRONG

Put each action in the right category:

CLEARLY WRONG:

- Stealing
- Hurting someone on purpose
- Lying to get someone in trouble
- Bullying
- Cheating on tests

IN-BETWEEN (DEPENDS):

- Telling a white lie
- Keeping a secret
- Breaking a rule to help someone
- Tattling on someone

CLEARLY RIGHT:

- Helping someone who's hurt
- Telling the truth
- Being kind
- Following rules that keep people safe
- Standing up for someone being bullied

PART 2: TRICKY SITUATION #1

Your friend tells you they're being bullied but makes you promise not to tell anyone.

- *What should you do? Why?*

PART 3: TRICKY SITUATION #2

You see someone drop $5 but they don't notice. No one else saw.

- *What should you do? Why?*

PART 4: TRICKY SITUATION #3

Your friend wants to copy your homework. They're really stressed and say they'll fail without it.

- *What should you do? Why?*

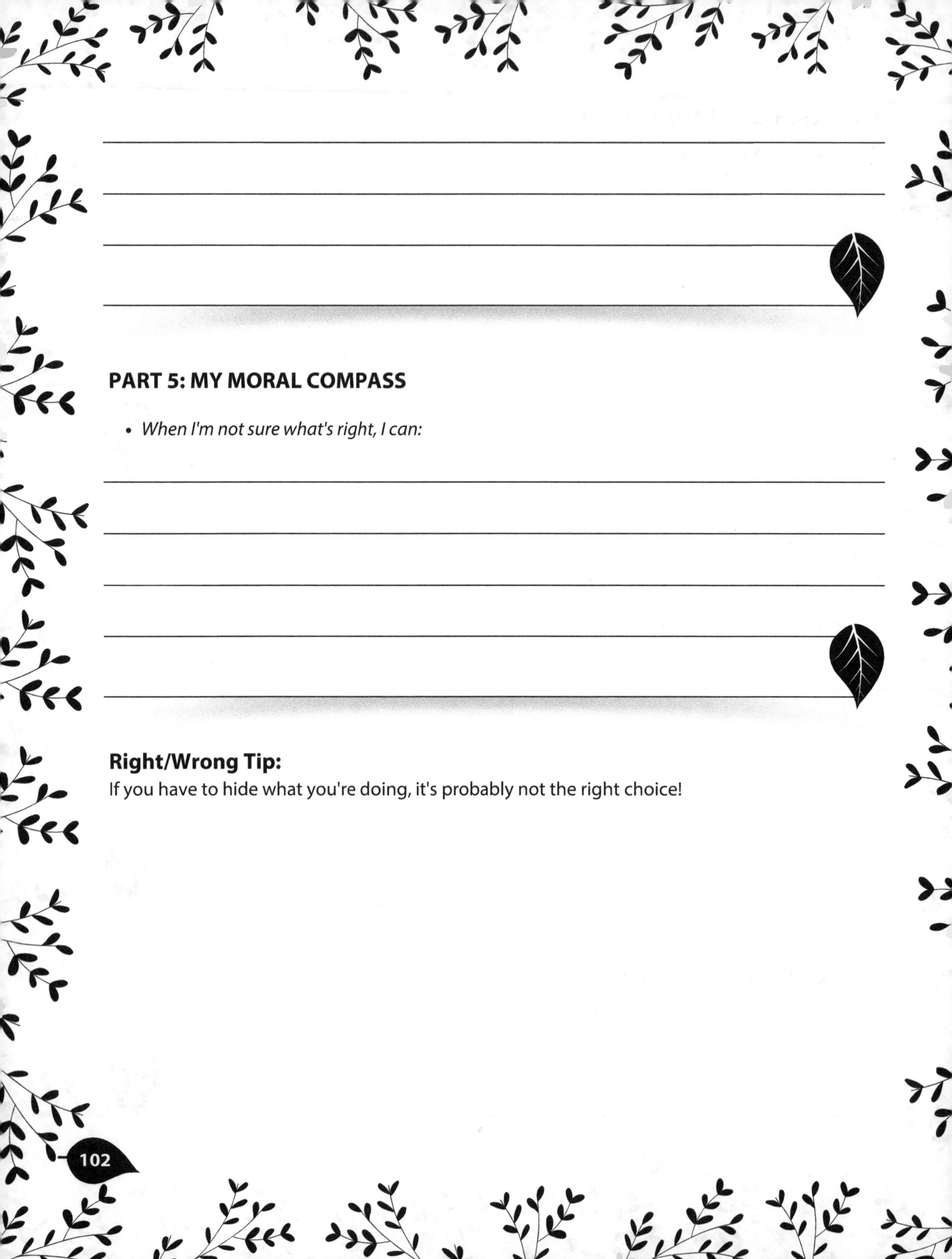

PART 5: MY MORAL COMPASS

- *When I'm not sure what's right, I can:*

Right/Wrong Tip:
If you have to hide what you're doing, it's probably not the right choice!

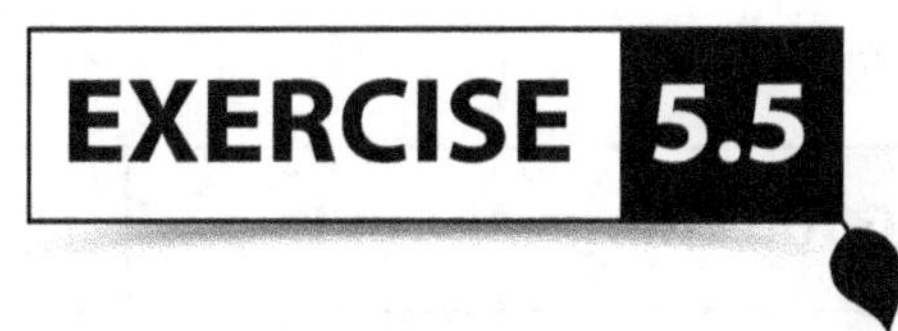

PLANNING MY SUMMER

Spring is when you plan for summer! Let's make good decisions about how to spend it.

PART 1: WHAT I WANT FROM SUMMER

Check your top 3 priorities

☐ Having fun

☐ Earning money

☐ Learning something new

☐ Spending time with friends

☐ Spending time with family

☐ Being active and outside

☐ Relaxing and resting

☐ Trying something new

☐ Going on adventures

☐ Reading and learning

☐ Playing sports

☐ Being creative

PART 2: SUMMER OPTIONS

Option	Good Things About It	Challenging Things About It
<u>Example:</u> Soccer camp	Learn new skills, make friends	Costs money, takes whole week

PART 3: THE PERFECT SUMMER BALANCE

Type of Activity	What I'll Do
FUN (playing, adventures)	
REST (relaxing, recharging)	
ACTIVE (sports, movement)	
LEARNING (camp, reading, skills)	

PART 4: SUMMER PLAN

- *My summer plan is:*

____

____ 

____

PART 5: WHAT I NEED TO DO NOW

- *To make my summer plan happen, I need to:*

____

____

____

____

____

Summer Tip:
Your summer doesn't have to be fancy to be good. Simple can be just as fun!

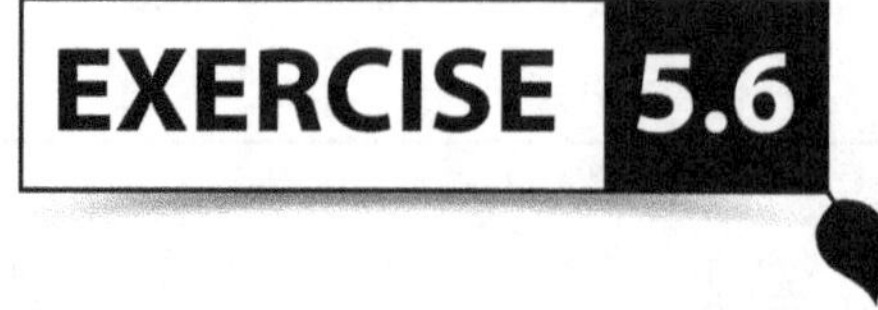

EXERCISE 5.6

TAKING CARE OF MY BODY AND MIND

Good choices about health help you feel your best!

PART 1: HEALTH CHECK

Healthy Habit	How Often Do I Do This? (Daily/Sometimes/Rarely)
Get enough sleep	
Eat healthy foods	
Drink water	
Move my body	
Play outside	
Take care of my teeth	
Wash my hands	
Limit junk food	

PART 2: ONE HABIT TO IMPROVE

- *The health habit I most want to work on:*

____

____

____

- *My plan:*

____

____

____

____

PART 3: SPRING HEALTH DECISIONS

Decision	My Choice
Movement: What activity will I do regularly?	
Sleep: What time will I go to bed?	
Food: What healthy food will I eat more?	
Outside: How often will I play outside?	

PART 4: WHAT HELPS, WHAT DOESN'T

Makes Healthy Choices EASIER	Makes Healthy Choices HARDER
<u>Example:</u> Having healthy snacks available	<u>Example:</u> Staying up late on screens

- *If I'm struggling with my health (physical or mental), I can talk to:*

____

____

____

____

____

Health Tip:

Small changes add up! Don't try to change everything at once.

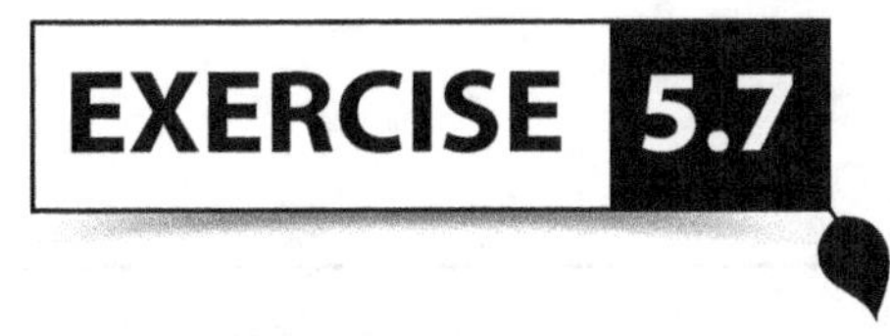

MY SPRING ACTION PLAN

This is it! Let's put everything together into one action plan for spring!

PART 1: LOOKING BACK

What did you learn from each chapter?

Chapter	One Thing I Learned
1: Self-Awareness	
2: Self-Management	
3: Social Awareness	
4: Relationship Skills	
5: Responsible Decision-Making	

PART 2: MY TOP 3 SPRING GOALS

1. ____

2. ____

3. ____

PART 3: ACTION STEPS

- *For each goal, what will you DO?*

Goal	Action Steps
Goal 1:	1. 2. 3.
Goal 2:	1. 2. 3.
Goal 3:	1. 2. 3.

PART 4: MY SPRING CALENDAR

Week	What I'll Focus On
This week	
Week 2	
Week 3	

Week 4	
Week 5	
Week 6	
Week 7	
Week 8	

PART 5: WHEN THINGS GET HARD

- *If I'm struggling or get off track, I will:*

____

____

____

____

____

PART 6: WHO WILL HELP ME

- *People who can support me:*

____

____

PART 7: MY SPRING PROMISE (REVISITED)

- *Remember your promise from Exercise 1.7? Let's update it!*

MY SPRING PROMISE

- *This spring, I promise to:*

____

____

____

____

____

____

Signed: _______________________________

Date: _______________________________

MAKE IT REAL:

Hang this somewhere you'll see it every day!

END OF CHAPTER 5: RESPONSIBLE DECISION-MAKING

YOU DID IT!

You finished all 5 chapters and 35 exercises!

- *What's the most important thing you learned from this workbook?*

____

____

____

____

____

____

Now What?

Keep using these skills! The more you practice, the better you'll get.

Turn the page for the conclusion...

CONCLUSION

KEEP GROWING!

Congratulations!

You just completed a LOT of work on yourself! That's something to be really proud of.

Through this workbook, you:

- Learned about yourself (Self-Awareness)
- Built skills to handle stress and reach goals (Self-Management)
- Practiced understanding and caring about others (Social Awareness)
- Worked on friendship and relationship skills (Relationship Skills)
- Got better at making good choices (Responsible Decision-Making)

What Happens Now?

The workbook is done, but your growth isn't! Keep using what you learned:

- Check in with your feelings regularly
- Use your calm-down tools when you need them
- Show kindness to others
- Work on your friendships
- Think before making decisions
- Keep working toward your goals

When Things Get Hard

You won't be perfect. Nobody is! You'll still:

- Get upset sometimes
- Make mistakes
- Have friend problems

- Make choices you regret

And that's okay! What matters is that you now have TOOLS to help you handle these things better.

Remember:

✓ You're always growing and learning
✓ It's okay to ask for help
✓ Small changes make a big difference
✓ You're capable of more than you think
✓ Your feelings are valid
✓ You matter!

Before You Go...

- *What's one thing you'll do differently because of this workbook?*

____

____

____

____

____

Keep growing, keep learning, and keep being awesome!

You've got this!

BONUS

QUICK HELP GUIDE

When I'm Feeling...

- **ANGRY:** Take deep breaths • Run around outside • Punch a pillow • Count to 10 • Draw angry pictures • Talk to someone
- **SAD:** Talk to someone you trust • Write in a journal • Listen to music • Hug a pet or person • Do something you enjoy • Cry if you need to
- **WORRIED:** Name what you're worried about • Deep breathing (5-finger breath) • Talk to a parent or teacher • Write it down • Remember times you handled hard things before
- **OVERWHELMED:** Make a list of what you need to do • Break big tasks into small steps • Do one thing at a time • Ask for help • Take a break
- **LONELY:** Reach out to a friend • Join an activity • Talk to family • Help someone else • Remember people who care about you
- **EXCITED:** Channel that energy! • Run, dance, move • Share your excitement • Plan for what you're excited about • Use excitement to motivate you

Quick Calm-Down Tools:

- **5-Finger Breathing:** Trace your hand, breathe in going up, out going down
- **5-4-3-2-1:** Name 5 things you see, 4 you feel, 3 you hear, 2 you smell, 1 you taste
- **Belly Breathing:** Hand on belly, breathe deep so belly goes out, then in
- **Count to 10** (slowly!)
- **Cold water** on face or hands

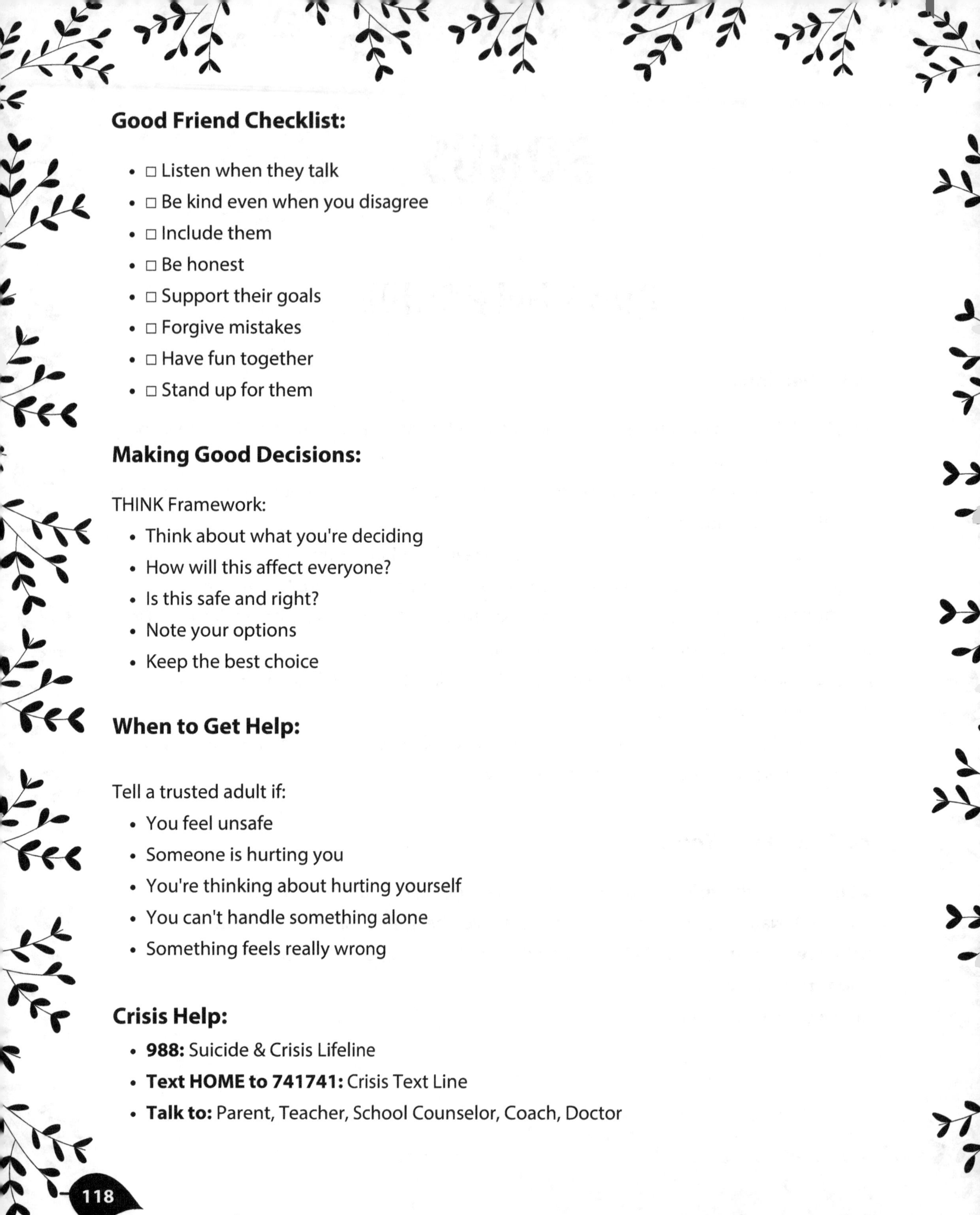

Good Friend Checklist:

- ☐ Listen when they talk
- ☐ Be kind even when you disagree
- ☐ Include them
- ☐ Be honest
- ☐ Support their goals
- ☐ Forgive mistakes
- ☐ Have fun together
- ☐ Stand up for them

Making Good Decisions:

THINK Framework:
- Think about what you're deciding
- How will this affect everyone?
- Is this safe and right?
- Note your options
- Keep the best choice

When to Get Help:

Tell a trusted adult if:
- You feel unsafe
- Someone is hurting you
- You're thinking about hurting yourself
- You can't handle something alone
- Something feels really wrong

Crisis Help:

- **988:** Suicide & Crisis Lifeline
- **Text HOME to 741741:** Crisis Text Line
- **Talk to:** Parent, Teacher, School Counselor, Coach, Doctor

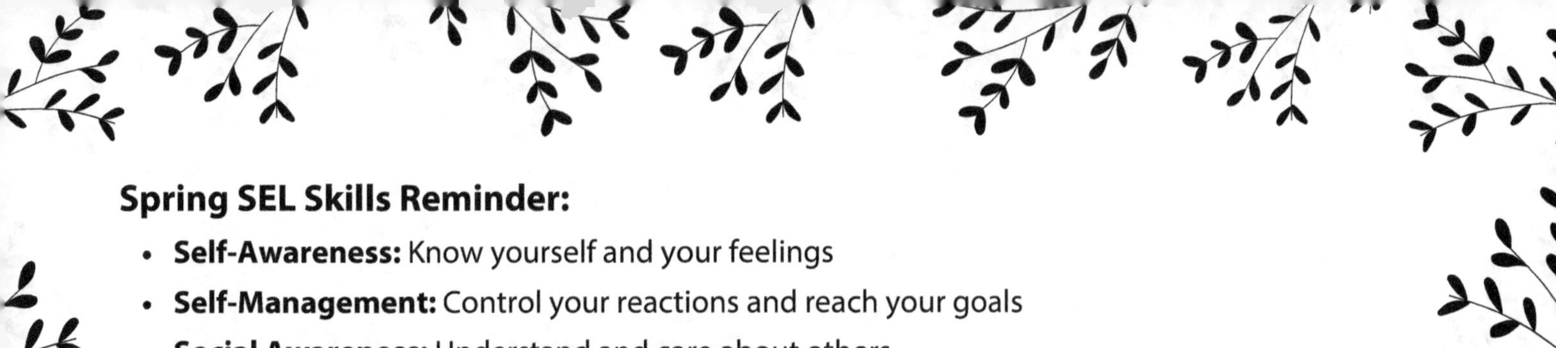

Spring SEL Skills Reminder:

- **Self-Awareness:** Know yourself and your feelings
- **Self-Management:** Control your reactions and reach your goals
- **Social Awareness:** Understand and care about others
- **Relationship Skills:** Get along well with people
- **Decision-Making:** Make smart, responsible choices

You've got the tools.

Now use them!

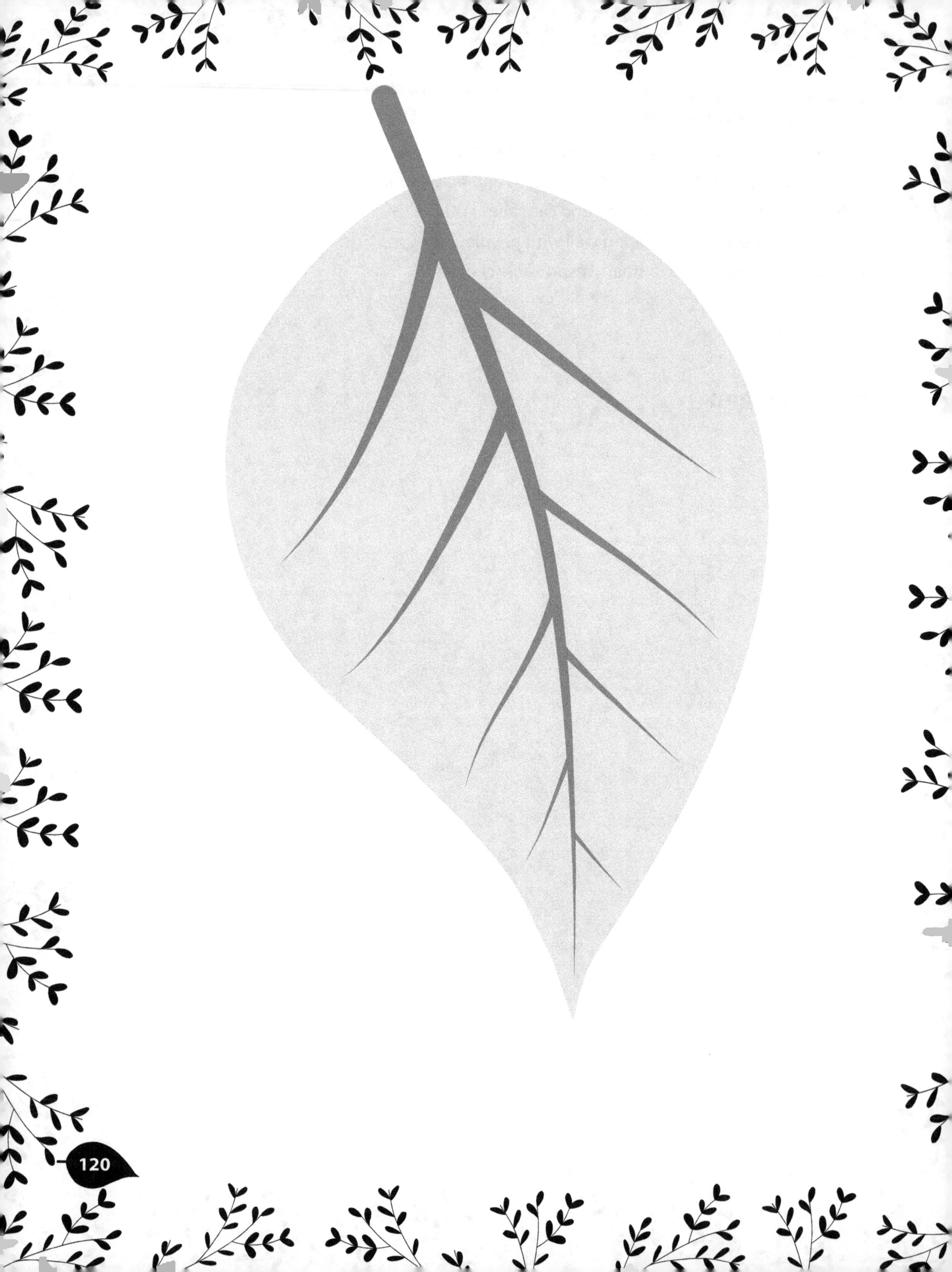

A MESSAGE FROM RICHARD BASS

Hey there!

Thank you for working through this workbook! I'm so proud of you for taking the time to learn about yourself and practice these important skills.

Why I Created This Book

I've been a teacher for a long time, and I've seen firsthand how much kids struggle when they don't have the tools to understand their feelings, manage stress, get along with others, and make good choices.

But here's the thing: These aren't skills you're born with. They're skills you LEARN. And that's exactly what you just did!

You're Not Alone

If some of the exercises were hard, or if you discovered things about yourself that you want to change that's normal! Everyone has stuff they're working on. The fact that you're willing to do this work means you're already on the right path.

Keep Going

This workbook is just one step in your journey. Keep practicing these skills. Keep being honest with yourself. Keep asking for help when you need it. Keep growing!

I'd Love to Hear From You

Did this workbook help you? What was your favorite exercise? What did you learn? You can share your thoughts at:

- **YouTube:** Thriving with Richard Bass

- **Instagram, TikTok and Facebook:** @richardbassauthor

- **Email:** richard@richardbassauthor.com

One More Thing...

If this workbook helped you, please ask your parent or teacher to leave a review on Amazon. Reviews help other kids find resources that might help them too!

Thanks for letting me be part of your spring growth journey. I'm cheering for you!

- Richard Bass

ABOUT THE AUTHOR

Richard Bass

Richard Bass is a well-established author with extensive knowledge and background on children's disabilities. He has also experienced first-hand many children and teens who deal with depression and anxiety. Richard also enjoys researching techniques and ideas to better serve students, as well as providing guidance to parents on how to understand and lead their children to success.

Richard wants to share his experience, research, and practices through his writing, as it has proven successful to many parents and students. He feels there is a need for parents and others around the child to fully understand the disability, or mental health of the child. He hopes that with his writing, people will be more understanding of children going through these issues.

In regards to his qualifications, Richard holds a bachelor's and master's degree in education as well as several certifications including Special Education K-12, and Educational Administration. Whenever he is not working, reading, or writing, he likes to travel with his family to learn about different cultures as well as get ideas from all around about the upbringing of children especially those with disabilities. He also researches and learns about different educational systems around the world.

Richard participates in several online groups where parents, educators, doctors, and psychologists share their successes with children with disabilities. He also has his own group where further discussion about his books and techniques take place. Apart from his participation in online groups, Richard also attends training related to the upbringing of students with disabilities and has also led training in this area.

3 FREE Bonuses!

- **Positive Discipline Playbook:** Dive into 50 powerful strategies designed to unleash your child's full potential through positive guidance. Say goodbye to tantrums and hello to harmony!

- **Kids' Planner:** Get organized and empower your child with this fun and interactive planner. From homework schedules to goal-setting, watch them blossom with confidence!

- **The Positive Self-Talk Guide:** Help your teen transform negative thoughts into powerful affirmations! This practical toolkit includes daily exercises, reframing techniques, and 50+ positive self-talk starters. Watch them shift from self-doubt to self-confidence!

REFERENCES

- **Cohen, J. (Ed.). (2001).** Caring classrooms/intelligent schools: The social emotional education of young children. Teachers College Press.

- **Cohen, L. J. (2001).** Playful parenting. Ballantine Books.

- **Collaborative for Academic, Social, and Emotional Learning. (2020).** What is SEL? https://casel.org/what-is-sel/

- **Durlak, J. A., Weissberg, R. P., Dymnicki, A. B., Taylor, R. D., & Schellinger, K. B. (2011).** The impact of enhancing students' social and emotional learning: A meta-analysis of school-based universal interventions. Child Development, 82(1), 405-432. https://doi.org/10.1111/j.1467-8624.2010.01564.x

- **Elias, M. J., & Arnold, H. (Eds.). (2006).** The educator's guide to emotional intelligence and academic achievement. Corwin Press.

- **Frankel, F. (2010).** Friends forever: How parents can help their kids make and keep good friends. Jossey-Bass.

- **Goleman, D. (1995).** Emotional intelligence: Why it matters more than IQ. Bantam Books.

- **Kaiser Greenland, S. (2010).** The mindful child: How to help your kid manage stress and become happier, kinder, and more compassionate. Free Press.

- **Mayer, J. D., & Salovey, P. (1997).** What is emotional intelligence? In P. Salovey & D. J. Sluyter (Eds.), Emotional development and emotional intelligence (pp. 3-34). Basic Books.

- **Siegel, D. J., & Bryson, T. P. (2011).** The whole-brain child: 12 revolutionary strategies to nurture your child's developing mind. Delacorte Press.

- **Thompson, M., & Barker, T. (2004).** It's a boy!: Your son's development from birth to age 18. Ballantine Books.

- **Willard, C. (2016).** Mindfulness for teen anxiety: A workbook for overcoming anxiety at home, at school, and everywhere else. Instant Help Books.